About Us

Who we are

The language services industry is growing and there is no end in sight. For your company to dominate the competition and be ahead of the game, you require insights – and that is exactly where we come in. We come from diverse backgrounds in the language industry. We are a market research and international consulting company made up of analysts, consultants, LSP experts, and researchers. But we are all connected with one united goal – Helping our clients succeed.

And yes. We know the industry.

What we do

With a global team management approach, we work directly with you, learning the ins and outs of your business so that we can help to customize and tailor your business needs on the global stage. When you localize your message to prospective global customers, you reach them on a much deeper level and that only means one thing – customers are engaged and interested. We help you to better understand and connect with your demographic.

We build actionable insights and reports that cater specifically to your products and services. We provide the window into the ever-changing translation and localization industries. Working with us means building relationships with influential players – an essential part of penetrating your market.

The future lies directly in the global market. We get inside the head of the localization users and focus on factors that are important to them. We research. We report. We advise. We direct. We guide.

We are here to help

Looking to move into the global market? Want to establish the ultimate customer experience? Need some insights into how to adapt your products and services to have the look and feel of your target market? Dreaming of creating an ultimate user experience – one that will help to advance your marketing strategy and drive your business goals?

We are here to help.

INFORMATION CONTAINED IN THIS REPORT

4 | RESEARCH TEAM

6 | THE NIMDZI 100

13 | CLOSE, BUT NO CIGAR

13 | WATCHLIST

16 | CHANGELOG

20 | HOW WE CREATE THE NIMDZI 100

22 | STATE OF THE LANGUAGE INDUSTRY

24 | MARKET SIZE AND GROWTH

40 | MERGERS, ACQUISITIONS, AND INVESTMENT IN 2021

42 | HOW BUYERS VIEW THE LSP LANDSCAPE

44 | KEY TRENDS

52 | SPOTLIGHT ON INDUSTRY SEGMENTS

62 | GEOGRAPHIES

66 | TURNING THE PAGE AFTER COVID-19

70 | HYPES AND BUZZWORDS: JUST SMOKE AND MIRRORS?

74 | WHERE DO WE GO FROM HERE?

TOP 100
LARGEST LANGUAGE SERVICE
PROVIDERS IN THE WORLD
Nimdzi
THE NIMDZI 100
2022

Research team

Sarah Hickey
Lead analyst and writer

Renato Beninatto
Chief advisor, Editor

Gabriel Karandyšovský
AI and localization, Editor

Belén Agulló García
Media and gaming

Yulia Akhulkova
Technology trends

Nadežda Jakubková
Geographies, Sustainability,
Data analysis

Hannah Leske
Women-run LSPs, Turning
the page after COVID-19,
Data analysis

Marina Ghazaryan
Data analysis

Nika Allahverdi
Marketing and outreach

Tucker Johnson
Co-Founder,
Advisor

Bobb Drake
Director of Geocultural
Research

Kristen Glant
Chief Financial Officer

Jonathan Otis
Director of M&A and
Growth Strategy

Josef Kubovsky
CEO

Inge Boonen
Chief Sales Officer

Aleksey Schipack
VP of Information
Technology

Rucha L. Sheth
VP of Customer
Success

Roman Civin
VP of Consulting

Marek Jakúbek
Localization Adviser

Miguel Sepulveda
Globalization
Specialist

Valeria Nanni
Localization
Specialist

Oscar Betancourt
Video Producer

Melissa Suarez
Marketing Communications
Analyst

Isabel Romero
Marketing
Coordinator

Paige Wastie
Marketing
Coordinator

**Christopher
Maitland-Walker**
M&A Advisor

Nicoli Potgieter
Sales Development
Representative

Laura Arias
Sales Development
Representative

Melissa Torres
VP Customer Success,
Americas

Petra Karandyšovský
Sales & Learning
Analyst

Alice Cain
Sales Development
Representative

Sean Louw
Sales Development
Representative

Dennis Rodriguez
Sales Development
Representative

Adriana Grande
International
UX Director

Rosemary Hynes
Interpreting
Researcher

THE NIMDZI 100

Chances are the information you came here for is the **Nimdzi 100 Ranking**, which is presented in the following table. The ranking is based on revenue and lists the top 100 largest language service providers (LSPs) worldwide.

Let's jump right in, shall we?

Rank	Company name	Country	2021 Revenue (USD million)	Note	Main business
01	TransPerfect	United States	1,110.0	v	translation, life sciences, legal
02	RWS	United Kingdom	955.3	fy	translation, patents, life sciences, IT
03	LanguageLine Solutions	United States	750.0	v	interpreting, translation & localization, healthcare, government
04	Keywords Studios	Ireland	596.9	v	video game services
05	Lionbridge	United States	545.9	v	translation, life sciences, technology, legal, games & entertainment
06	Iyuno-SDI Group	United States	450.0	v	media localization
07	Appen	Australia	447.3	fy	data company
08	translate plus	United Kingdom	353.4	v	translation, dubbing, manufacturing, marketing
09	Acolad Group	France	307.3	v	translation & localization, manufacturing, life sciences, government
10	Welocalize	United States	299.0	v	translation & localization, linguistic staffing
11	Hogarth Worldwide	United Kingdom	260.0	v	communications company, localization
12	Poletowin Pitcrew Holdings	Japan	243.4	fy	translation, video game services
13	STAR Group	Switzerland	195.8	v	translation & localization, platform licensing, automotive & aviation, manufacturing
14	Pactera EDGE	United States	193.0	v	localization, data curation, global experiences
15	Pixelogic Media	United States	186.0	e	media localization

16	AMN Language Services	United States	181.0	fy	interpreting, healthcare
17	CyraCom International	United States	174.8	v	interpreting, translation, healthcare, insurance, government
18	Translation Bureau	Canada	153.3	v	translation & localization, interpreting, government
19	President Translation Service Group International (PTSGI)	Taiwan	130.0	v	translation & localization, interpreting, healthcare, video games, financial & legal, life sciences
20	Dubbing Brothers	France	112.3	v	dubbing & audio, subtitling, media & entertainment
21	Voice and Script International (VSI)	United Kingdom	103.1	v	media localization
22	GTCOM (Global Tone Communication Technology)	China	91.5	v	language technology, translation, data & AI
23	Honyaku Center	Japan	90.2	v	translation, patents, life sciences, finance & legal
24	thebigword	United Kingdom	89.7	e	interpreting, translation, government
25	United Language Group	United States	88.0	v	translation, interpreting, healthcare, life sciences
26	STAR7	Italy	86.3	e	translation & localization services, manufacturing, IT
27	Ubiqus	France	83.1	v	translation, finance, technology, legal, life sciences
28	Morningside	United States	80.3	e	translation, legal, patents, life sciences
29	LanguageWire	Denmark	75.2	v	translation, life sciences, luxury, automotive
30	Vistatec	Ireland	74.5	e	translation, LQA
31	BIG Language Solutions	United States	74.0	v	translation, interpreting, education, legal, healthcare, life sciences, financial
32	SWISS TXT	Switzerland	68.7	v	media localization
33	Logos Group	Italy	63.0	v	translation & localization, copywriting & transcreation, dubbing & audio
34	SeproTec Multilingual Solutions	Spain	60.9	v	translation, interpreting, pharma, life sciences, IP
35	ZOO Digital Group	United Kingdom	57.0	v	subtitling, dubbing, media & entertainment

36	KERN Global Language Services	Germany	56.9	v	translation, interpreting, life sciences, automotive, technology, financial
37	Verztec	Singapore	56.0	v	interpreting, transcription, DTP & graphic design, education, financial & legal
38	Sunyu Transphere	China	55.8	v	translation & localization, intellectual property, technology & IT
39	Hiventy	France	55.2	e	subtitling, dubbing & audio, media & entertainment
40	Certified Languages International	United States	55.1	v	interpreting, healthcare, other LSPs
41	Translated	Italy	53.2	v	translation & localization, tourism, technology
42	MotionPoint	United States	50.0	v	website translation
43	Språkservice Sverige	Sweden	48.6	v	interpreting, translation & localization, government, technology & IT
44	Akorbi	United States	47.5	v	healthcare, financial, interpreting
45	Prime Focus Technologies	India	46.0	v	media localization
46	Global Talk	Netherlands	45.4	v	interpreting, government, healthcare
47	Argos Multilingual	United States	43.5	v	translation & localization, life sciences, technology & IT
48	EC Innovations	Singapore	43.0	v	translation & localization, interpreting, life sciences, technology & IT
49	Uphealth-Martti	United States	41.0	v	interpreting, healthcare
50	ONCALL Language Services	Australia	39.4	e	interpreting, healthcare
51	CQ fluency	United States	38.4	v	translation & localization, healthcare, life sciences
52	CSOFT International	United States + China	38.0	v	translation & localization, interpreting, technology & IT, life sciences
53	Rozetta	Japan	37.6	c	translation, platform, technology
54	Akagane	Japan	37.3	v	translation & localization, DTP & graphic design, manufacturing
55	Alpha CRC	United Kingdom	37.0	v	technology & IT, video games, translation & localization

56	Ai-Media	Australia	36.5	fy	translation & localization services, government, education
57	CRESTEC — Localization	Japan	35.1	v	translation, localization, manufacturing, automotive, IT & software
58	Apostroph Group	Germany	33.9	v	translation & localization, marketing, life sciences
59	Propio Language Services	United States	33.2	v	healthcare, government
60	Valbin Corporation	United States	32.6	e	government
61	PGLS	United States	32.4	v	translation & localization, government
62	Traductions Serge Bélair (TRSB)	Canada	32.1	v	translation & localization, financial & legal, life sciences
63	Plint	Sweden	30.8	v	media localization
64	MasterWord Services	United States	30.4	v	linguist staffing, interpreting, translation & localization, government, healthcare
65	Spark	United Kingdom	29.9	e	localization, technology, media
66	GLOBO Language Solutions	United States	29.8	v	interpreting, healthcare, government, education
67	Straker Translations	New Zealand	29.1	v	technology & IT, manufacturing, translation & localization
68	EVA	France	28.8	v	dubbing, media localization
69	Versacom	Canada	28.5	v	translation & localization, financial & legal
70	Janus Worldwide	Austria	28.5	v	translation & localization, technology & IT, manufacturing
71	Multicultural NSW	Australia	28.0	fy	translation, interpreting, government
72	Sichuan Lan-bridge Information Technology Co.	China	27.6	v	translation & localization, manufacturing, technology & IT, automotive
73	Acclaro	United States	27.5	v	translation & localization, copywriting & content creation, technology & IT, media & entertainment
74	Summa Linguae Technologies	Poland	27.4	v	data & AI, translation & localization, technology & IT
75	Transvoice	Sweden	26.8	v	interpreting, healthcare, government

76	t'works	Germany	26.1	v	translation, website localization, manufacturing, life sciences, legal
77	Skrivanek	Czech Republic	25.1	v	translation & localization, manufacturing, other LSPs
78	BLEND	Israel	25.0	v	translation & localization, education, IT, video games
79	Capita Translation and Interpreting	United Kingdom	24.8	e	translation, interpreting, legal
80	Transline Gruppe	Germany	23.5	v	translation & localization, DTP & graphic design, manufacturing, life sciences
81	THG Fluently	United Kingdom	23.3	e	translation & localization, copywriting & content creation, consumer goods, beauty & wellness
82	Supertext	Switzerland	21.5	v	translation, transcreation, marketing
83	Glodom Language Solutions	China	21.0	v	translation, IT, patents
84	CBG Konsult & Information	Sweden	21.0	v	translation & localization, automotive & aviation, government
85	LanguageLoop	Australia	19.9	e	interpreting, government
86	DA Languages	United Kingdom	18.7	v	interpreting, translation, education, financial
87	Lingsoft Group	Finland	17.1	v	translation & localization, government, other LSPs
88	24translate Group	Germany	16.8	v	translation & localization, DTP & graphic design, financial & legal
89	mt-g	Germany	16.5	v	translation & localization, DTP & graphic design, life sciences
90	kothes GmbH	Germany	16.3	v	translation & localization services, technology, DTP & graphic design
91	Awatera	Cyprus	16.0	v	translation & localization, interpreting, life sciences, technology & IT, gaming
92	e2f	United States	14.8	v	data & AI, translation, linguist staffing, technology
93	TOIN Corporation	Japan	14.7	v	transcreation, translation, technology & IT, creative services
94	German Translation Network - Ge|Tra|Net|	Germany	14.5	v	translation & localization, interpreting, manufacturing, financial & legal
95	EVS Translations	Germany	14.4	v	translation, finance, legal
96	Human Science	Japan	14.3	v	translation & localization, data & AI, technology & IT, marketing
97	Interpreters Unlimited Group	United States	14.0	v	interpreting, legal, education, gaming
98	Hansem Global	South Korea	13.5	v	technical writing, translation, consumer goods
99	itl Institut für technische Literatur	Germany	13.0	v	translation & localization, automotive & aviation, technology & IT
100	Presence Translate & Interact	Luxembourg	12.6	v	interpreting, healthcare, government

Our ranking is a live document and is therefore subject to change.

Notes

fy   **fiscal year**, figures for the latest financial year (verified with financial reports)

v   **verified**, data provided by companies

e   **estimated revenue**, based on extensive industry research

c   **calculation** based on public financial records

•   Some companies may appear to have the same revenue due to currency rounding. However, the ranking order is accurate considering the second decimal.

Close, but no cigar

The following companies would have made the ranking in previous editions, but due to the growth of other players, as well as new arrivals on the Nimdzi 100, they did not make the cut this year. However, they deserve an honorable mention.

Company name	Country	2021 Revenue (USD million)	Note	Main business
Linguava	United States	12.0	V	interpreting, translation & localization, healthcare
Mondia Technologies Ltd	United Kingdom	11.7	V	translation & localization, retail, legal
Kaleidoscope	Austria	11.2	V	translation & localization, transcreation, manufacturing
Global Lingo	United Kingdom	11.2	V	translation, interpreting, transcription, technology & IT, e-learning
Ingenuiti	United States	11.0	V	translation, DTP & graphic design, life sciences
Andovar	Thailand	10.7	V	education, video games, retail
tolingo GmbH	Germany	10.5	V	translation & localization, technology & IT
Fidel Softech	India	10.5	V	translation, localization, technology
Sandberg Translation Partners	United Kingdom	10.2	V	Work for other LSPs

Watchlist

Language service providers without a definitive revenue estimate

The Watchlist consists of companies that should be in the ranking but are not listed because they do not disclose, publish, or otherwise reveal their revenue. Furthermore, some organizations are units inside larger corporate groups where a small part of revenue comes from language services, and annual reports do not allow researchers to segment out the translation and interpreting revenue. We provide visibility to such companies on the Watchlist to highlight their impact on the industry.

The reason it is important for us to track these companies is because, even though they might not compete for clients, they compete for talent and resources. They also represent opportunities for technology providers and investors.

The companies are listed in alphabetical order.

Company	Headquarters	Description
Ability InterBusiness Solutions (AIBS)	Japan	translation, technical writing
Advanced Language Systems International	United States	translation, localization, government
Alibaba Language Services	China	IT company, translation platform
AllWorld Language Consultants (ALC)	United States	translation, interpreting, government
American Language Services (AML-Global)	United States	translation, interpreting, legal, technical, media
Angel Translation Corporation	China	translation, localization, interpreting
CALNET	United States	government, interpreting
Chizai Corporation	Japan	translation, patents
Conduit Language Specialists	United States	translation, interpreting, government
Congress Global Communications	Japan	translation, interpreting, conference
CWU	United States	translation, interpreting, government
Datawords	France	translation, marketing
Deluxe	United States	media localization
Diction	Switzerland	translation & localization, marketing, financial & legal
DXC ACG	United States	IT company, translation, software localization
EasyTranslate	Denmark	interpreting, translation, government
EnVeritas Group (EVG)	United States	communications company, content localization
Geneva Worldwide	United States	interpreting, translation, legal, healthcare
Global Linguist Solutions (GLS)	United States	translation, interpreting, government
ICON	Ireland	clinical research group, life sciences, translation
IDC Digital	United States	media localization
Iota Localization Services	Ireland	translation & localization, IT and software, education, security
Jonckers	Belgium	translation platform
Language Services Associates	United States	interpreting, healthcare, insurance, financial
Leidos	United States	translation, interpreting, government
Lingo24	United Kingdom	translation, platform, technology
LIS Solutions (Legal Interpreting Solutions)	United States	interpreting, government
LocTeam	Spain	translation, localization

Company	Headquarters	Description
Maruboshi Co., part of CMC Corporation	Japan	translation, interpreting, technical writing
Metropolitan Interpreters and Translators (Metlang)	United States	translation, interpreting, government
Mid Atlantic Professionals (SSI)	United States	government, interpreting
Mission Essential	United States	translation, interpreting, government
Mother Tongue	United Kingdom	transcreation, translation, content creation
MultiLingual Solutions (MLS)	United States	translation, interpreting, software localization
MVM	United States	translation, interpreting, government
Pactera Technology	China	translation & localization, language testing & QA, technology, IT & software
Qloc	Poland	localization, video game services
Raytheon	United States	government, language technology
Smartling	United States	IT company, translation, content localization
Sorenson Community Interpreting Services	United States	sign language interpreting
SOS International	United States	translation, localization, interpreting, government
SunFlare	Japan	translation, technical writing
Testronic	United Kingdom	video game services, localization
TITRAFILM	France	media localization
Toppan Digital Language	United Kingdom	translation & localization, healthcare, marketing, finance
Tradutec Group	France	translation, life sciences, finance
TranslateMedia	United Kingdom	translation, retail, media
Transn	China	translation, financial & legal
tsd GmbH	Germany	translation, manufacturing, financial, pharma
Visual Data Media Services	United States	media localization
WCS Group	Netherlands	translation, interpreting, technical documentation
Wordbank	United Kingdom	translation, audiovisual, marketing
WordTech International	China	translation, localization
WorldWide Language Resources	United States	translation, interpreting, government
Yamagata	Japan	documentation company, technical translation
ZVRS / Purple Communications	United States	sign language interpreting

Changelog

A lot has changed on the ranking since last year. Here is a brief overview to help you better navigate the ranking.

New arrivals on the Nimdzi 100

translate plus
UK-based translate plus is one of Europe's top language service providers by revenue. The company has a diversified client base, specializing in the manufacturing and marketing industries. translate plus used to be on our Watchlist in previous editions but was never featured in the ranking. This year the company officially disclosed their figures to us and skyrocketed right to the top.

$353.4 MILLION

Hogarth Worldwide
Hogarth Worldwide is a communications company based in the United Kingdom. The company has been on our Watchlist for some time and officially disclosed their figures to us this year.

$260.0 MILLION

Poletowin Pitcrew Holdings
Poletowin Pitcrew Holdings is a Japanese company specializing in translation and video game localization. The company was on our Watchlist in previous editions and features in the ranking for the first time this year.

$243.4 MILLION

AMN Language Services
After acquiring Stratus Video in 2020, AMN Language Services was moved to our Watchlist in the 2021 ranking. This year they are back, holding position 16 in the 2022 ranking.

$181.0 MILLION

GTCOM (Global Tone Communication Technology)
GTCOM is based in China. The company specializes in language technology and AI solutions. GTCOM was on our Watchlist in previous years and officially disclosed their figures to us this year.

$91.5 MILLION

STAR7
Italian STAR7 acquired Ireland-based LocalEyes (previously on our Watchlist) in 2021, helping boost the company to position 26 in this year's ranking. STAR7 operates in many verticals but is particularly focused on the fields of manufacturing and IT.

$86.3 MILLION

Ai-Media

$36.5 MILLION

Ai-Media is an Australian company which specializes in captioning and translation services. The company is most active in the public sectors, especially government and education.

PGLS

$32.4 MILLION

PGLS is based in the United States and is one of just a few minority-owned companies in the 2021 ranking. The company offers translation and localization services in the public sector. PGLS is an absolute newcomer to the Nimdzi 100 ranking, seeing as the company grew to more than ten times its size in just one year, via a mix of acquisitions and organic growth.

EVA

$28.8 MILLION

EVA is headquartered in France, with several offices across western Europe. The media localization company focuses on audiovisual accessibility solutions such as dubbing, captioning and subtitling.

DA Languages

$18.7 MILLION

DA Languages is a translating agency based in the United Kingdom. The company is most active in the education and finance verticals.

kothes GmbH

$16.3 MILLION

kothes GmbH is a translation and localization company based in Germany that focuses on technical documentation and information solutions. The company also offers consulting and content creation.

German Translation Network - Ge|Tra|Net|

$14.5 MILLION

Ge|Tra|Net| is, predictably, a German translation company. The company offers translation, localization and interpreting services to a number of industries, but is particularly focused on manufacturing and finance.

Presence Translate & Interact

$12.6 MILLION

Presence Translate & Interact is an interpreting company headquartered in Luxembourg. The company specializes in healthcare and government interpreting services.

Rebranded

Iyuno Media Group rebranded in 2021 to reflect its acquisition of SDI Media. The company is now known as **Iyuno SDI Group.**

Cloudbreak-Martti was number 49 in our 2021 ranking. Since then, Cloudbreak merged with UpHealth and is now trading under UpHealth Inc. This year the company is listed as **Uphealth-Martti** in the ranking. We added "Martti" to the name to make reference to the company's well-known interpreting platform.

Acquired and removed from the ranking

SDL is an industry veteran and has been featured on every previous edition of the Nimdzi 100. In 2021, the company ranked fourth, with an estimated revenue of **USD 480.7 million.** SDL was acquired by **RWS** at the end of 2020 and is therefore no longer listed individually in our ranking.

SDI Media held position number 10 in the 2021 ranking, with a confirmed revenue of **USD 191 million**. SDI Media was acquired by **Iyuno Media Group** in 2021, and **Iyuno-SDI Group** was formed.

Semantix held position 27 in the 2021 ranking, with a confirmed revenue of **USD 73.7 million.** Semantix was acquired by **TransPerfect** last year and no longer appears individually in the ranking.

LanguageLink ranked 62nd last year, with a confirmed revenue of **USD 27 million**. **BIG Language Solutions** acquired the company in 2021, so the LanguageLink brand has been removed from the ranking.

Next Level Globalization (NLG) held position 71 last year, with a revenue of **USD 22.2 million.** It was acquired by **Welocalize** in July 2021 and is no longer listed individually in our ranking.

How we create the Nimdzi 100

During the course of this market analysis, Nimdzi uncovered prominent LSPs that have previously been invisible in market reports because they do not participate in surveys and are reluctant to disclose their revenue. **Nimdzi has employed an investigative approach and invested hundreds of hours into intense research, data collection, and analysis in order to present data that have previously been unavailable.**

We are very proud to offer broad access to our data. This ranking is offered to all who are interested. No paywall. No strings attached. Localization buyers, investors, savvy job seekers, and analysts are welcome to use this document. *Just don't forget to reference Nimdzi Insights, LLC, as the source.* Interested parties are free to **reach out to us directly** should they have any questions.

Below is a summary of the methodology used for the Nimdzi 100 ranking.

01 **We concentrated on identifying LSPs with USD 10 million or more in revenue,** with the assistance of in-country experts. In most countries, there are only a few providers of this size, and it is impossible for them to hide from local competitors because they hire staff, take part in requests for proposals and employ a large number of translators. Once we identified the relevant LSPs, we researched information that could help us make more accurate estimates of their size and talked to the management directly to verify our findings.

02 **We're listing full company revenue, not just language services revenue.** It is impossible to separate these in external sources of information, such as annual reports, press releases, and stock listings, which provide the foundation for our work.

03 **We use data from the latest fiscal year for each company.** This means the numbers for some companies will not reflect 2021 calendar year revenues.

04 **Our definition of language services includes:** translation, localization, transcreation, multilingual desktop publishing (DTP), language quality assurance, linguistic testing, multilingual copywriting, multilingual technical writing, language project management, interpreting, video remote interpreting, telephone interpreting, linguist verification and staffing, media localization, versioning, adaptation, subtitling, voiceover, dubbing, machine translation (MT), training machine translation engines, cultural consulting, data services, and related services.

05 **Growth rates are calculated in USD.**

06 **We use average annual currency conversion rates to US dollars,** published by the Internal Revenue Service of the United States for each day of trading in 2021.

State of the language industry

At this point in time, we are two years into the COVID-19 pandemic and our analysis shows that many of the new trends we observed in 2020 solidified in 2021.

When the pandemic first hit, language service providers (LSPs) had to act fast to adapt their business models to the new environment and meet their clients' changing needs. Companies of all sizes increased their digital offerings, added new platforms, features and services, restructured their internal operations, worked on integrations, and received completely new types of requests that fueled innovation. It was stressful, it was scary, it was exciting. We can say without exaggeration that the pandemic kicked off a new chapter for the global labor market and that things will never return to the way they were before March 2020.

Fast forward to 2022, it seems the language services market is better set up than ever before to meet the increasingly complex demands of buyers and is reaping the rewards of the efforts put in at the start of the pandemic. That the language services industry is coming out stronger is reflected in the strong growth the top 100 LSPs experienced in 2021 — through both mergers and acquisitions (M&A) and outside investment, as well as via organic growth.

It is fair to say that 2021 was an exceptionally great year for the language industry and that factors such as a backlog demand (from the 2020 lockdowns) in sectors like government and media, as well as the continued boom in e-commerce and e-learning heavily contributed to this fact. However, even after this exceptional year, we can expect that the industry will continue to grow at a faster pace than before. The global market has changed, and at this point in time LSPs have adapted well to it and are ready to meet and exceed the new requirements. We have long said that our industry is impervious to crises. The latest developments show that what significantly contributes to this resilience is the incredible agility of the individual companies in the market.

Throughout this report, we reference different data points that were used for our analysis. In some cases, we report directly about data relating to the top 100 largest LSPs. In other cases, our calculations are based on data collected via our survey, which received 167 valid responses from LSPs of all sizes (including about two-thirds of the top 100 from our ranking). We also refer back to data collected via interviews we conducted with more than 30 of the largest players in the language industry. We highlight the sources of our data where appropriate.

Market size & growth

Our data show that annual growth among the 100 largest LSPs has increased significantly. Between 2020 and 2021, the combined revenues of the top 100 positions in our ranking increased by 22.7%, compared to only 6.8% in the previous period.

The combined revenue of the companies comprising the top 10 positions in 2021 rose 23.3% compared to the top 10 listed in 2020. The strongest growth was experienced by the segment of companies comprising the top 20 positions, whose combined revenues increased by 24.8% as compared to those holding the top 20 positions last year. The top 50 positions grew by 23.2% and the remaining positions 51 to 100 grew by 19.1%, as compared to last year's ranking.

Growth by ranking segment between 2020 and 2021

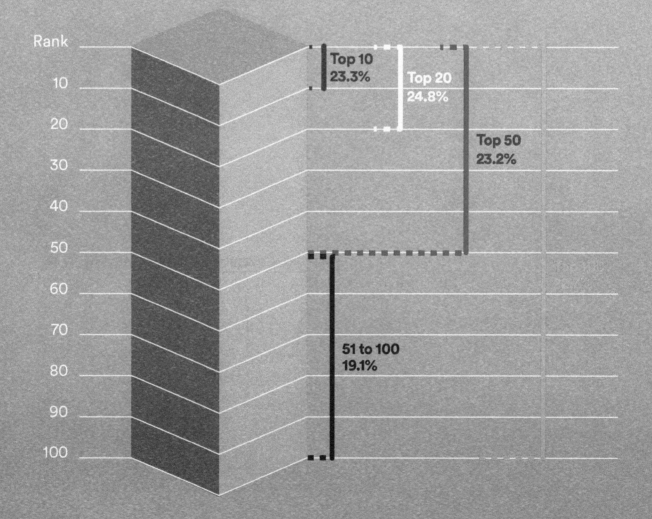

Growth by ranking segment, two-year comparison

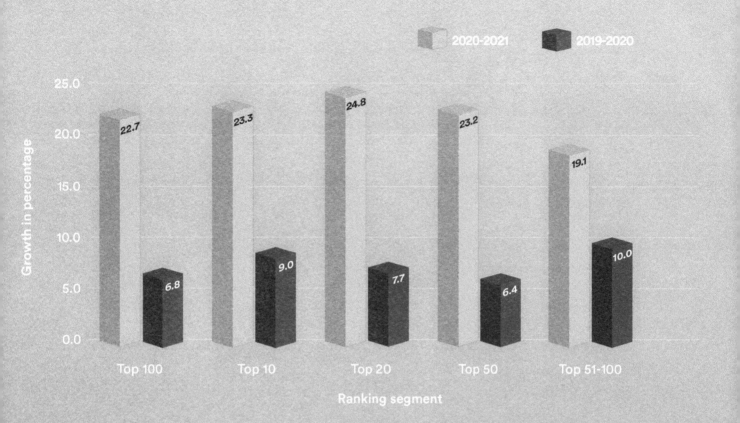

Legend: 2020-2021 (light), 2019-2020 (dark)

Y-axis: Growth in percentage
X-axis: Ranking segment

- Top 100: 22.7, 6.8
- Top 10: 23.3, 9.0
- Top 20: 24.8, 7.7
- Top 50: 23.2, 6.4
- Top 51-100: 19.1, 10.0

Revenues of the top 100 ranking positions from 2017 to 2021

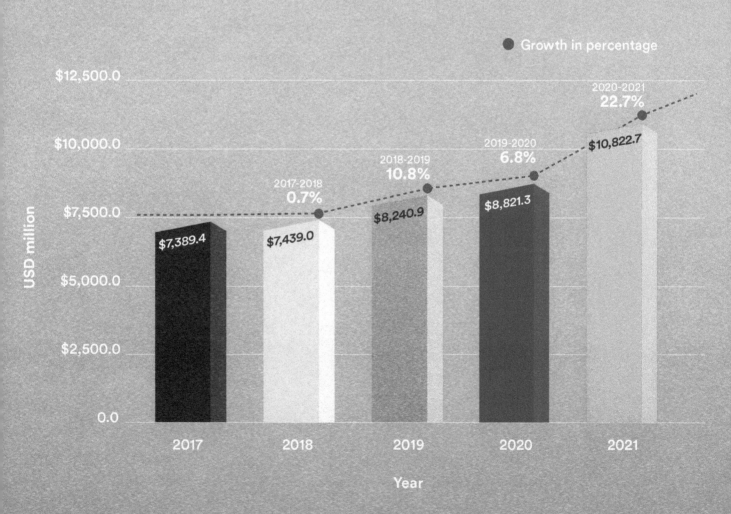

● Growth in percentage

Y-axis: USD million
X-axis: Year

- 2017: $7,389.4
- 2018: $7,439.0 — 2017-2018 0.7%
- 2019: $8,240.9 — 2018-2019 10.8%
- 2020: $8,821.3 — 2019-2020 6.8%
- 2021: $10,822.7 — 2020-2021 22.7%

The first billion-dollar company

Despite ongoing consolidation at the top, the industry as a whole continues to grow, producing larger LSPs every year. This trend holds true even in the lowest positions within our ranking, with the 100th largest LSP confirming revenues of USD 12.6 million this year as compared with USD 12.0 million, USD 11.6 million and USD 10.3 million for the 100th ranked LSPs in 2020, 2019 and 2018, respectively.

For the first time, the language industry now has a billion-dollar company. Long-time industry leader TransPerfect reached USD 1.1 billion in revenue in 2021. This is up from USD 852.4 million in 2020 and represents an increase of more than 30% year-over-year. Especially for a company of this size and during times that saw the world economy suffer, this is an impressive level of growth.

In last year's Nimdzi 100 we reported that RWS became the new de facto leader in the industry after its acquisition of former rival SDL. Back then, in March 2021, the combined 2020 revenues of RWS and SDL stood at USD 937.5 million and outperformed TransPerfect by USD 85.1 million, which indicated a shift in leadership at the top. However, TransPerfect made a strong comeback and solidified its position as the largest LSP in the world once again — partially also through the acquisition of industry veteran and Nordic leader Semantix, whose revenue stood at USD 73.7 million in 2020.

Given the acquisition of former rival SDL, which propelled RWS to the top, the company was expected to reach the billion dollar mark in 2021. However, the newly combined company only grew by a little less than two percent in 2021, reaching USD 955.3 million. A possible explanation could be a focus on aligning company efforts after the mega acquisition and a change in leadership — in June 2021, RWS announced the appointment of a new Group CEO, Ian El-Mokadem, who replaced Richard Thompson at the helm.

Lionbridge, another household name in the market, held the position as the second-largest language service provider for many years. In 2020, the company sold its AI division — Lionbridge AI — to TELUS International, a digital customer experience company from Canada. The deal went through for approximately USD 935 million (CAD 1.2 billion). Despite the sale, Lionbridge is not leaving this lucrative field altogether but will rather focus its AI efforts exclusively on language services, for instance in the form of neural machine translation (NMT) as well as using applied AI to tag, annotate and score content to drive automation and improve quality checks and cost estimates in the translation workflow. In this year's ranking, Lionbridge made it to the 5th position, with USD 545.9 in revenue.

In order to gain some perspective of growth and consolidation in the industry, we decided to take a look at the revenues of the top two positions in our ranking based on revenues from 2017 to 2021.

The two largest LSPs in the world from 2017 to 2021

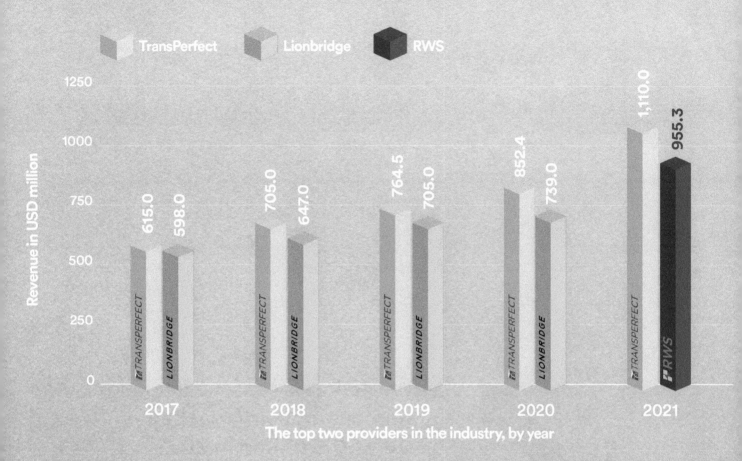

Revenue in USD million

TransPerfect   Lionbridge   RWS

Year	TransPerfect	Lionbridge / RWS
2017	615.0	598.0
2018	705.0	647.0
2019	764.5	705.0
2020	852.4	739.0
2021	1,110.0	955.3

The top two providers in the industry, by year

What the graph shows is by how much the two largest positions in the industry have grown in only five years. Between 2017 and 2021, the number one position in the language industry (consistently held by TransPerfect) grew by more than 80% and the second position (previously Lionbridge, now RWS) grew by close to 60%. Put differently, if we consider the compound annual growth rates (CAGR) for the two top positions in our ranking, the growth was at least twice as fast as for the rest of the industry (15.9% and 12.4%, versus 6.0%).

Size of the market and five-year growth projection

Last year, we had reduced our growth estimate to reflect the impact of the pandemic, adjusting the market's compound annual growth rate (CAGR) to 6.0%, down from 6.2% and 6.8% in previous years. However, 2021 was a phenomenal year that saw LSPs of all sizes reporting record growth, which we accounted for in this year's projection.

We estimate that the language services industry reached **USD 60.5 billion** in **2021** and should grow to **USD 64.7 billion** in **2022**.

Our estimate for 2021 reflects a one-off increase of 10% compared to 2020. Going forward, our estimate is slightly more conservative knowing that the industry just went through two exceptional years — one that caused a strong slow-down and one that saw a big push in demand, partially due to the 2020 backlog. While it is unrealistic to expect this exceptional level of growth to continue, we can expect that the industry will continue to grow at a faster pace than before March 2020, thanks to a changed market that LSPs have adapted well to at this point in time. This is why we project a CAGR of 7.0% for the coming years. Taking this into account, the industry would be valued at USD 84.9 billion by 2026.

Five year growth projection

When calculating the addressable market for their services, commercial providers should limit the opportunity to 60% of the total figure. Firstly, not everything is outsourced, as a significant portion of the overall volume is performed by in-house teams on the buyer side. For example, the European Union employs about 5,000 staff translators and interpreters. Secondly, the market size calculation includes revenues for both translation companies and their suppliers, i.e. a part of the revenue is counted twice.

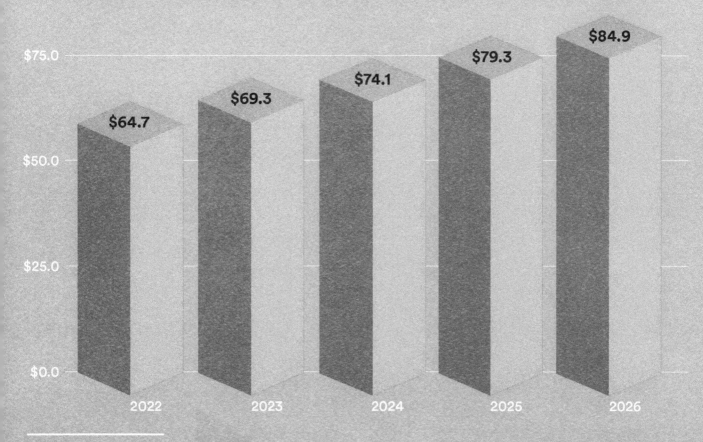

Market volume
USD billion

Top 100 companies concentrate 17.9% of industry revenue

Although consolidation continues, the language services industry remains fragmented. The top 100 companies in our ranking accounted for just 17.9% of the overall language industry in 2021 — a rise of 1.9% from 2020. Adding in the Watchlist and our "Close, but no cigar" honorary ranking, all 165 large LSPs tracked by Nimdzi accounted for only 22.8% of the language industry in 2021.

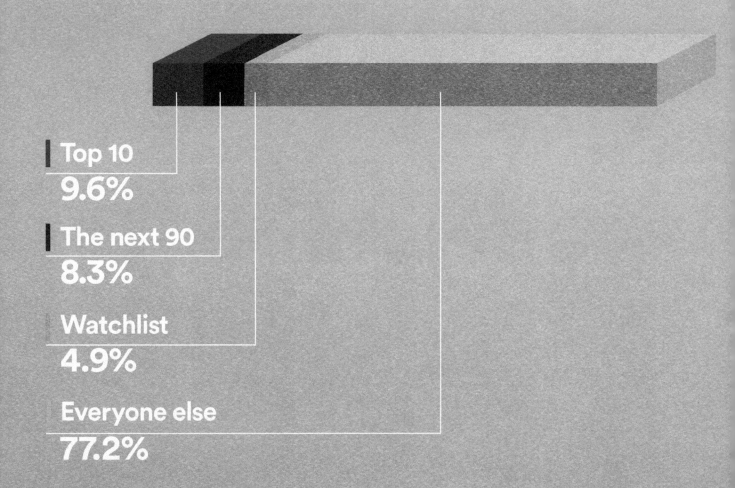

Top 10
9.6%

The next 90
8.3%

Watchlist
4.9%

Everyone else
77.2%

In absolute figures, the companies tracked by Nimdzi earned over USD 13.8 billion in their latest fiscal years. The top 10 companies were responsible for more than 40% of that total.

❚ USD 5.8 billion in the top 10

❚ USD 5.0 billion in the next 90

❚ USD 3.0 billion approximately on the Watchlist (including the "Close, but no cigar" honorary ranking for this purpose)

Despite ongoing consolidation at the top, the industry is still predominantly made up of companies smaller than USD 10 million.

A closer look at the top 100

In this year's ranking, 86 of the top 100 largest LSPs in the world reported various degrees of growth, 10 companies had negative growth, and revenue remained flat for one company. This is a big change from last year, where only 65 companies from the top 100 reported positive growth, 33 had negative growth, and revenues remained flat for two companies on the ranking.

We typically report on the average growth of the top 100 by revenue bracket. However, this year, there is one company (PGLS) that significantly skews the picture, as they grew by more than 1,300% (see "*The 10 fastest-growing LSPs in our ranking*"). Given that this is such a significant outlier, we decided to calculate the median growth per ranking segment this year, to allow for a more accurate picture.

The median growth rate for the top 100 in this year's ranking was 15.3%, up from 5.1% in 2020. In last year's ranking, both the top 20 and the top 50 grew at a median rate of 5.0%, whereas companies on the same positions in this year's ranking reported a median growth rate of 15.9% and 14.3% respectively. The biggest growth by ranking segment can be found at the very top and at the very bottom: The median growth of this year's top 10 was 18.1% (compared to 7.9% in 2020), which is still slightly topped by LSPs in ranks 51 to 100 with 18.2% — 12.3% higher than the previous period.

Median growth of the top 100 in 2020 and 2021, by revenue bracket

	2020 median growth	2021 median growth	Change
Top 100	5.1%	15.3%	10.2%
Top 10	7.9%	18.1%	10.2%
Top 20	5.0%	15.9%	10.9%
Top 50	5.0%	14.3%	9.3%
Top 51-100	5.9%	18.2%	12.3%

Growth by company size

When calculating the growth by company size we again opted for the median instead of the average to allow for a more accurate picture given the significant outlier in this year's ranking (PGLS).

Looking at the results, companies with 50 to 99 employees came out on top, with a median growth rate of 21.6%. In last year's ranking, it was the same company size class that grew the most, however, the median then was only 10.7%, so there's an increase of more than 10% this year for the same group. Next in line were LSPs with 100 to 249 employees, who recorded a median growth rate of 17.6% in 2021 — up nearly 10% from 2020.

The data show that growth was strong across all company sizes last year. To illustrate, the slowest positive growth rate was reported for companies with 500 to 999 employees. This group still came out at 13.1%, which is 2.4% more than last year's frontrunner. These results are another clear reflection of the tremendous year the language services industry had in 2021.

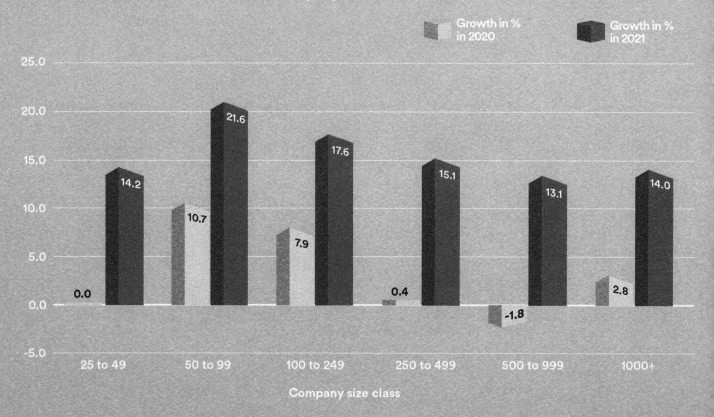

The most productive companies in the industry

Looking at the productivity of the top 100 LSPs, the average revenue per employee in 2021 was about USD 213 thousand. In 2020, the average was USD 102 thousand, so this is an increase in productivity of about 109%. The average productivity for the top 20 was USD 202 thousand in 2021. It is worth noting that only one company from the top 10 in our ranking is among the ten most productive companies. Aside from translate plus, none of the top 40 LSPs in our ranking made it onto this list.

Considering company size, seven out of the ten most productive companies in 2021 employ between 25 and 99 professionals. Two companies in this ranking have between 100 and 249 full-time employees. The most productive company — translate plus — has between 250 and 499 people on staff. None of the most productive companies employ 500 people or more.

It is also worth noting that there is an overrepresentation of interpreting companies in this list. Five out of the ten most productive companies in 2021 — Språkservice Sverige, Global Talk, LanguageLoop, Interpreters Unlimited Group, and GLOBO Language Solutions — all derive a large portion of their revenue from interpreting services. It is possible that the move to remote interpreting contributed to the increase in productivity for these companies.

Rank	Company	Productivity (USD per employee)	2021 Revenue (USD million)	Size class
1	translate plus	1,104,462	353.4	250 to 499
2	Språkservice Sverige	823,369	48.6	50 to 99
3	Global Talk	698,309	45.4	50 to 99
4	PGLS	675,000	32.4	25 to 49
5	Plint	640,727	30.8	25 to 49
6	LanguageLoop	496,622	19.9	25 to 49
7	Interpreters Unlimited Group	466,667	14.0	25 to 49
8	Translated	454,628	53.2	100 to 249
9	GLOBO Language Solutions	445,013	29.8	50 to 99
10	MotionPoint	423,729	50.0	100 to 249

The 10 fastest-growing LSPs in our ranking

Below is a list of the ten fastest-growing LSPs in 2021. The significant growth experienced by the top 100 and the industry at large was due to a perfect storm of strong M&A activity as well as organic growth fuelled by a backlog in demand from 2020.

We also need to highlight that the company that experienced the fastest growth by far — PGLS — represents an absolute outlier in our data. In 2021, the company grew more than ten times its size due to a mix of acquisitions and organic growth.

Rank	Company	Growth %	Revenue (USD million)	Core business
1	PGLS	1,308.7	32.4	translation & localization, government
2	GTCOM (Global Tone Communication Technology)	145.1	91.5	language technology, translation, data & AI
3	MasterWord Services	141.6	30.4	linguist staffing, interpreting, translation & localization, government, healthcare
4	Propio Language Services	125.9	33.2	healthcare, government
5	RWS	109.2	955.3	translation, patents, life sciences, IT
6	Ai-Media	108.7	36.5	translation & localization services, government, education
7	Vistatec	104.0	74.5	translation, LQA
8	German Translation Network - Ge|Tra|Net|	96.2	14.5	translation & localization, interpreting, manufacturing, financial & legal
9	Argos Multilingual	86.1	43.5	translation & localization, life sciences, technology & IT
10	BIG Language Solutions	80.5	74.0	translation, interpreting, education, legal, healthcare, life sciences, financial

Women-run LSPs

This year, 17 companies in our ranking are women-owned or women-run. The number fell from 20% in 2021, but still places our industry well above the global average of 8.2% (according to the Fortune 500). The majority of these women-run companies are based in North America, followed closely by Europe (nine and seven, respectively), and one company is based in Asia (two, if we consider CSOFT International's dual US and China headquarters).

Rank in the top 100	Company	Country	2021 Revenue (USD million)	Note
18	Translation Bureau	Canada	153.3	v
40	Certified Languages International	United States	55.1	v
44	Akorbi	United States	47.5	v
46	Global Talk	Netherlands	45.4	v
47	Argos Multilingual	United States	43.5	v
51	CQ fluency	United States	38.4	v
52	CSOFT International	United States + China	38.0	v
55	Alpha CRC	United Kingdom	37.0	v
60	Valbin Corporation	United States	32.6	e
61	Traductions Serge Bélair (TRSB)	Canada	32.1	v
64	MasterWord Services	United States	30.4	v
80	Transline Gruppe	Germany	23.5	v
82	Supertext	Switzerland	21.5	v
86	DA Languages	United Kingdom	18.7	v
89	mt-g	Germany	16.5	v
98	Hansem Global	South Korea	13.5	v
99	itl Institut für technische Literatur	Germany	13.0	v

As much as we want to laud the progress in our industry and congratulate these women on their achievements, it is also important to highlight the distance we still have to go. Although 17% of companies are women-led, only 6.1% of the total revenue of Nimdzi's top 100 is generated by these LSPs. Furthermore, there are again no female CEOs among the top 10 largest companies in the industry. The distribution is far from equal and we hope to see this gap narrow in 2022.

Nimdzi would like to especially mention the achievements of Translation Bureau's Lucie Séguin. For the second year running, Lucie is the only female CEO of a Nimdzi top 20-ranked company, and the only woman to lead a company with revenues above USD 150 million.

Top services and verticals in the market

In this year's survey, we asked companies to select the services and verticals they operate in.

The results show that the services most commonly provided by LSPs are *translation and localization* (98.1%), *machine translation and post-editing* (79.0%), *subtitling* (71.3%), and *copywriting, transcreation, content creation* (61.1%). *Dubbing, voiceovers and audio services* and *desktop publishing and graphic design* are in fifth place (60.5% each). *Transcription* is in sixth place (58.0%), *onsite interpreting* (51.0%) and *remote interpreting* (49.0%) moved to seventh and eighth place respectively.

The results are fairly consistent with last year's data, although the percentages changed slightly. Most notably, the number of companies providing *machine translation and post-editing* increased by 7.5%, and *copywriting, transcreation, content creation* moved ahead of *desktop publishing and graphic design* — confirming the push for original content creation we're highlighting in the trends section of this report.

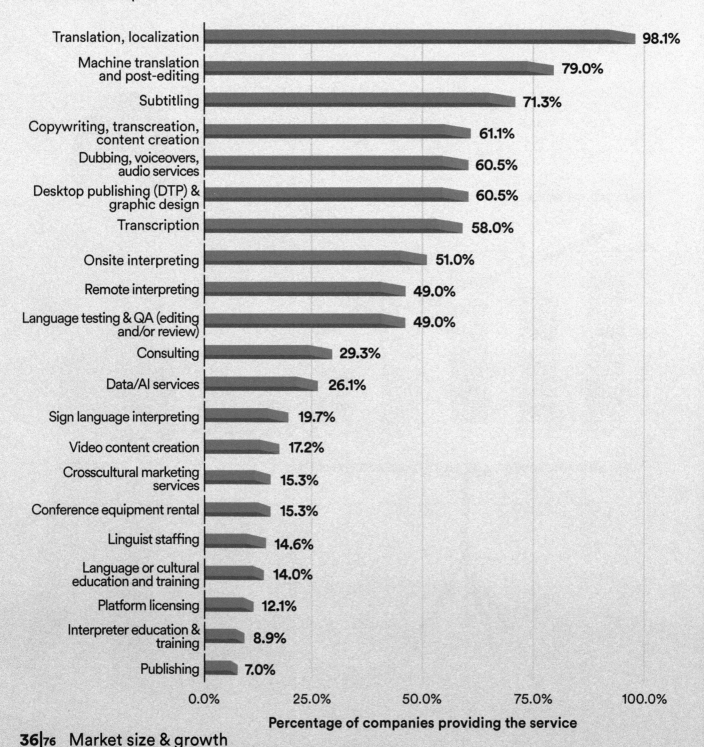

Percentage of companies providing the service

Considering the split by verticals, our survey results show that *technology, IT & software* (67.3%), *financial and legal* (65.4%), and *marketing* (60.4%) are the three most prevalent segments in terms of industry participation. This is a change from last year, where *life sciences* was in third place with 67.7% of survey respondents being active in this segment. This year *life sciences* is in fourth place with 60.4% listing this industry in their portfolio.

Education & e-learning (57.9%) and *manufacturing* (56.6%) are the fifth and sixth most common industry segments, with *government* reaching the seventh place (61.5%). *Media & entertainment* is in eighth place (49.1%).

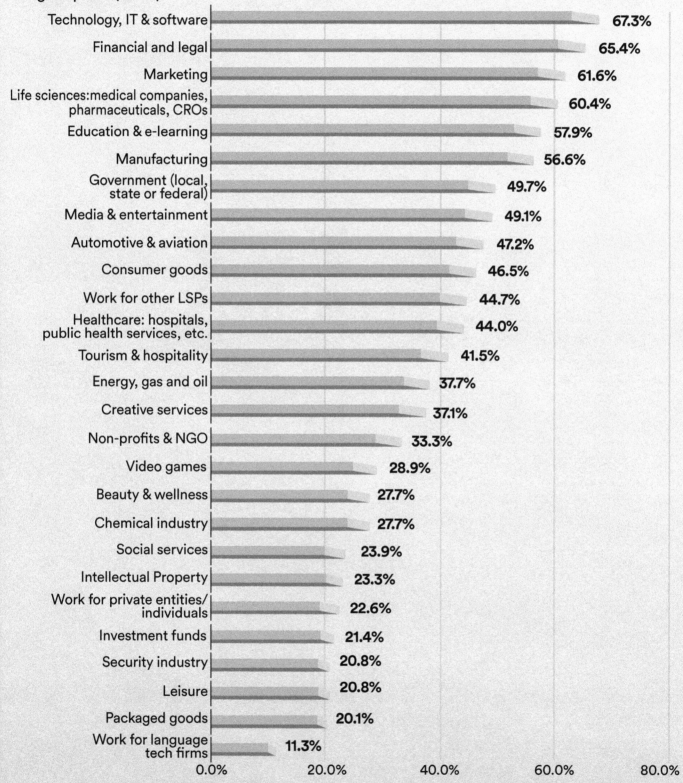

Percentage of companies active in each industry segment

When looking at these data it is important to bear in mind that these results represent a numerical count, showing how many players offer a certain service or operate in a certain vertical. They do not reflect the market share by revenue.

Growth by geographical distribution

North America
19.7%

To get a better sense of where the biggest growth came from by geographical distribution in 2021, we have compiled a map of the growth rates of the top 100 LSPs by region, based on country headquarters. We are again using the median growth rate to counteract the otherwise skewed picture caused by one company with above average growth.

We calculate growth based on revenues expressed in USD, using the annual exchange rate for each day of trading. This means that, for some regions, currency fluctuations skew the growth picture. For example, EUR, GBP, AUD, CAD and SEK performed better against USD in 2021 than they did in 2020, so as a result, companies reporting in these currencies saw a boost to growth in the equivalent USD. On the flipside, in comparison to 2020, companies reporting in JPY and RUR saw a negative impact from currency fluctuations in 2021.

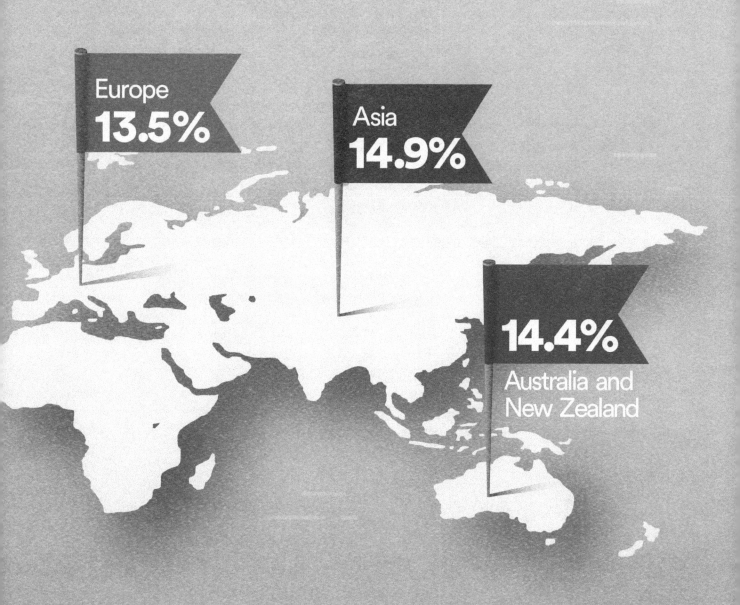

Mergers, acquisitions, and investment in 2021

The M&A and investment wave we highlighted in last year's Nimdzi 100 continued to gain momentum in 2021. In fact, what began as a trend is starting to resemble a frenzy and the industry now finds itself in a vicious circle of growth. While at first glance it is the number of deals that stands out, a closer look reveals that the real story is about the significantly increased valuations of the individual firms.

Over the last two years, there has been so much M&A and investment activity that the number of companies available for purchase started dwindling. The decreasing supply of mid-sized LSPs has created a real seller's market that has incentivized the remaining medium-sized players to sell their businesses at prices that would have been unimaginable and unacceptable a mere half year ago. These blown-out-of-proportion deals are now drawing even more attention to the industry and investors are flocking to the market to get a piece of the pie.

But it doesn't stop there — because, of course, investors do not invest to stay the same, they invest for growth. As investors are looking for returns and putting pressure on LSPs to deliver, the fresh money that is pouring into the market continues to feed the M&A wave. Why? Because acquisition has become the easiest and fastest way to grow. Especially as the links between LSPs and enterprise buyers are tightening via strategic partnerships (see "Key trends" section of the report), it has become more difficult for other LSPs to come in and snatch up a client from the competition. The much easier way is to simply buy the competition and get the clients by default.

Fuelled by the pressure to please investors, LSPs continue to buy up the mid-market segment, regardless of price. Once strategic, the M&A activity has turned into a sink or swim situation — keep up or go home, accept the price or leave empty-handed.

As the growth circle continues, we can expect it to have a knock-on effect on the wider dynamics of the market. For instance, as the companies receiving funding have money to spend, this will not only impact M&A but also recruitment and technological development. In addition, in some cases the ROI pressure has created start-up-style issues around money, resources, and client retention, which are commonly experienced by businesses in Silicon Valley but are relatively new to the language industry.

While PE-firms were already heavily investing in the language industry prior to 2020, they kept it rather quiet. Over the last two years this has changed and the PE community has become far more visible in the language services space. If we look at the top 100 companies in our ranking, 30 are currently backed by private equity or venture capital — that's close to half of all privately-owned LSPs on the list (61). Given the latest developments, we can expect this figure to grow.

Looking at M&A, our data confirm that the buying trend is far from over. In the survey for this year's Nimdzi 100, 45.7% of respondents stated that they are looking for companies to acquire, which is up 12.0% in comparison to last year's results. In addition, 26.4% are looking to sell, which is an increase of only 2.5% as compared to 2021 (confirming once more that there are fewer companies that want to sell than want to buy). In the same vein, the number of companies stating they are not thinking about M&A at all has decreased by 8.2%.

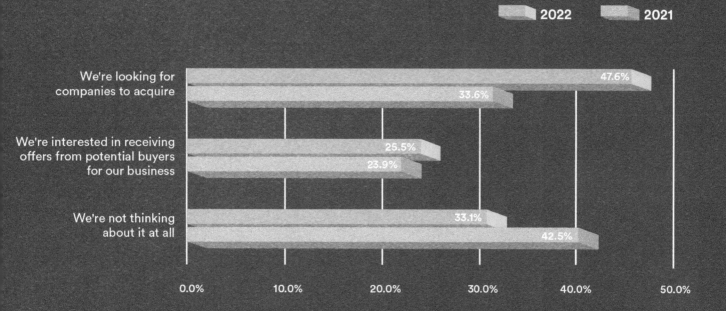

How buyers view the LSP landscape

What the ranking doesn't show is that many of the top providers in the industry are not in direct competition with one another. Because the market is so fragmented, there are many clusters of top players for the various sectors within the language services industry.

While companies from the top ranks are trying to diversify and branch out into other segments, no one, for example, comes near Keywords Studios when it comes to gaming, near Iyuno Media Group when it comes to media localization, or near LanguageLine Solutions in the area of interpreting.

In every segment of the market, there are a handful of LSPs that have reached the level of brand awareness that puts them in a top-of-mind position for buyers. From a buyer's point of view, the top companies in each segment of the industry are more likely to be bundled and tend to be interrelated in the client's mind. Let's take a look at who they are, per sector of the industry.

01
TRANSLATION AND LOCALIZATION

- TransPerfect
- RWS
- Lionbridge
- Welocalize

02
MEDIA LOCALIZATION

- Iyuno-SDI Group
- VSI
- ZOO Digital Group
- Deluxe

03
GAME LOCALIZATION

- Keywords Studios
- Poletowin
- Lionbridge

04
INTERPRETING

- LanguageLine Solutions
- CyraCom International
- thebigword
- AMN Language Services (formerly Stratus Video)

05
DATA AND IT

- Appen
- Pactera EDGE

Key trends

Considering the ranking of top players, the Watchlist of significant market influencers, as well as numerous briefings with industry experts, we highlight a number of current key trends and challenges we identified throughout the course of our analysis.

The Great Renegotiation

Broadly speaking, no matter what industry you're in, there are only three ways to grow your business:

- Acquiring new clients
- Selling more to existing clients
- Increasing prices

The first two ways listed are the ones businesses in the language industry typically tend to focus on in their growth strategies. It's the third option that often gets overlooked. But maybe not for much longer because time has come to talk about price increases.

The supply chain in the market seems to have reached its bottom level of pricing and shows signs that a significant adjustment in rates is imperative. Every year, large LSPs go through rounds of negotiation with their in-country suppliers trying to achieve margin gains by requiring reductions in rates in exchange for potential additional volume or based on hypothetical productivity gains. The reality is that often neither of these materialize.

By Nimdzi's estimation, depending on language-pair and subject matter area, prices are lagging between 11% and 20%. In some cases, like German, Italian, and Brazilian Portuguese (in combination with English), translation rates might be as much as 25% lower than what they should be.

Several factors drive the need for a realignment of prices:

- **Inflation.** From appliance stores in the United States to food markets in Brazil and gas stations in Poland, rising consumer prices fueled by high energy costs and supply chain disruptions are straining families and small businesses all over the world. Rising inflation is leading to price increases for food, gas, and other products and pushing language professionals to choose between digging deeper into their pockets or tightening their belts.

- **Record-high corporate profits.** A report from financial data firm FactSet found that the blended net profit margins for companies in the S&P 500 reached 12.9% in the third quarter and 12.0% in the fourth quarter of 2021. FactSet noted that Q3 2021 marked the second-highest net profit margin for the index, following only the record-breaking 13.1% margins posted in the second quarter of 2021. Nimdzi's research shows that over 45% of the revenues of the S&P 500 companies comes from international sales.

- **Inconsistent technology-driven productivity gains.** The proliferation of language technologies (as indicated by the mind-boggling 770 tools mapped in Nimdzi's Language Technology Atlas) might falsely imply potential productivity improvements, but the nature of the language business is such that a translator works for several clients and is required to master multiple technologies to make a living. These jack-of-all-trades report that their productivity levels are, in fact, negatively impacted by the multiple environments in which they are required to work.

Why renegotiate?

The theory is that renegotiation is generally triggered for one of two reasons: an imperfect contract or changed circumstances. If profits from clients are soaring and international sales are increasing while resources are becoming scarce and productivity gains are often fictitious (they can be achieved in simulations but not necessarily in real life), it is time to talk about price renegotiations. The circumstances have changed.

As with many other things in life, what prevents change is fear. On one hand, LSPs are afraid to ask clients for price increases and on the other, localization managers are afraid to ask for budget increases for their organizations. This is because translation/localization is seen as a cost to be managed, instead of an investment to be nurtured.

LSPs don't know how to explain value, and localization managers are not prone to associating their contribution to their companies' international success or just keep doing things the way that they have always been done. Nimdzi recently completed an extensive audit for a client, and was able to find USD 4 million in savings just in internal process improvements.

This insecurity sets the stage for driving cost pressures down the supply chain. It is also what will ultimately drive translators out of the business, and companies will be scrambling for talent down the line. Talent takes time to develop, and talent needs to be selected, trained, and managed.

 Even though LSPs invoice words, what they sell is project management and talent development. LSPs manage complexity, and complexity is hard to automate.

If translators aren't paid enough, they will find other jobs or decide to stop working and go back to school. If single-language vendors are not paid enough, they will reduce the quality of service because they cannot achieve decent margins. If multilanguage vendors are not paid enough they will resort to delivering whatever their computers can automate. Until the house of cards starts to crumble because of a single mistranslated word.

The talent shortage and the Great Resignation

Which brings us to another, closely related topic: The talent shortage in the industry.

While volumes keep rising and turnaround times are getting tighter, LSPs from all sides of the market are reporting that talent acquisition and talent retention are two of their biggest challenges in 2022.

As already pointed out in the previous section that talks about a need for price increases, professionals are leaving the industry due to low rates and poor working conditions. On the other end of the spectrum, large LSPs are complaining about a lack of qualified linguists to fill the rising demand. In the media localization sector, this topic even went mainstream after a TikTok influencer complained about the poor quality of the closed captions in Netflix show Squid Game.

While talk of a talent shortage in the language industry is nothing new, it appears to have reached a boiling point. What is also important to note is that it's a multifaceted challenge:

Finding the right people for the right price: In interviews for the Nimdzi 100, some LSPs reported that they cannot hire as fast as the demand is growing. This is particularly true in media localization where companies experienced a flood of requests once COVID-19 restrictions loosened and production was able to resume. Others said the problem is not with finding people but with not being able to afford them. Many LSPs have partnerships with universities as a way to have better access to new talent. However, especially as students graduate with high-level degrees, salary expectations often do not match what LSPs are willing or able to pay.

Talent retention: The talent shortage does not exclusively apply to linguists but also to other roles, such as sales and project management. A number of companies on the top 100 highlighted that they lost quite a few good people to client-side companies outside the language industry. Particularly to large tech firms who were able to make more lucrative offers. Because while LSPs have been undercutting one another for a long time, large enterprises are not willing to cut corners and can afford to hire the best people for the right price.

The right people at the right time: The talent shortage is particularly prominent for certain language pools. All too often, demand for less common language combinations rises and falls quite abruptly. For instance, when several clients suddenly want to scale up in the same region at the same time. During these hyper growth spurts, the demand is condensed and incredibly high for certain languages at a certain time. The two main challenges that arise out of this are finding enough qualified linguists to fill the demand on short notice, and then not being able to keep these people around once the projects are completed due to the enormous fluctuations in demand for these less common languages.

Changing roles: As volumes are increasing, budgets are tightening, and talent is scarce, LSPs are trying to increase automation as much as possible in an effort to reduce costs and increase efficiency. What this also means is that the roles of linguists are changing to better fit into this new environment. There is an assumption that people can buy post-editing relatively cheaply. However, this is not what translators want. Typically, translators don't get excited about the prospect of correcting MT output. Of course, the majority of translators use MT, but rather as just another tool in their translation process. So there is a misalignment between what the market needs and what linguists want and can provide. (P.S.: Paying post-editors based on how many corrections they make is not helping the situation.)

Location doesn't matter anymore - or does it?: Since the onset of the pandemic and the subsequent move to remote work, location doesn't matter anymore. Anyone can work from anywhere and businesses can hire talent all over the world. But it's not as simple as that. For some businesses, the shift to remote work increased their struggle for talent retention. For instance, when companies based in the capitals of nations started hiring people remotely, offering better jobs and capital wages, businesses located outside the capital were losing good people who previously were dependent on finding jobs in the cities they were based in. On the other hand, for companies based in the same cities as large tech players, being able to hire remotely has reduced the likelihood of employees being snatched up by enterprise clients located in the same area.

The Great Resignation

The Great Resignation is typically discussed in relation to the US workforce, but the phenomenon is international. In interviews for the Nimdzi 100, LSPs from around the world reported having lost people to the Great Resignation. While some are leaving over working conditions, low pay, or better career opportunities, that's not all there is to it.

Interestingly, reports include employees resigning for reasons such as wanting to go traveling for a few years, embracing their freedoms, and focusing on what really matters in life, outside of work. It is likely that this trend was accelerated by the pandemic as people worldwide had their freedom of movement restricted and had time to rethink what they wanted. The overall phenomenon of the Great Resignation paired with the more industry-specific developments highlighted above has brought the talent challenge to a whole new level. It is no longer the exception but something that is happening at scale.

Over time, the supply chain constraints will drive the trend toward higher rates. In addition, Nimdzi believes that this period will trigger the creation of a new generation of resources coming from diverse and unexpected backgrounds that will need to be trained from scratch. Already in the past few years, we have learned of remote staff based in places like Guatemala, Cambodia, Dominican Republic, Cape Verde, Turkey, and Zambia, to name but a few. This could potentially also increase demand for schools to develop this talent within the industry.

LSPs, understandably, tend to focus on the value they bring to their clients. However, maybe time has come to also focus on highlighting the value they bring to their staff, especially their linguists.

The new LSP: Highly-personalized, data-driven, and unafraid to venture beyond the confines of language services

In last year's edition of the Nimdzi 100, we declared that the LSP is dead. Meaning that at least the largest players in the industry are outgrowing the traditional, transaction-based LSP concept. Instead, what we are observing is that LSPs are increasingly becoming strategic partners and advisors for their clients' global business.

Based on interviews with the top 100 this year, it has become clear that this transition not only continued but was heavily accelerated in 2021. So much so that we can now talk about the era of a new kind of LSP — one that is trying to shed this very same acronym and instead grow the "strategic" and "partnership" dimension of its client relations.

To explain what exactly we're talking about, we're going to break it up into the different sub-segments of the overarching theme we've identified.

It's all about the end-user: Content creation and xLQA

In interviews, companies from the top 100 largest LSPs repeatedly mentioned a major push from clients for original content creation. This trend has been steadily on the rise for a while now and appears to have become one of *the* biggest opportunities for LSPs to tap into.

What stands out is that, reportedly, the discussions between LSPs and buyers are moving away from talking about translation and localization, and toward zeroing in on the best way to reach end-users. Enterprise clients are realizing that for their content to have the desired impact on their target audience, having it translated is (in many cases) not enough anymore. As the world is becoming more connected and people are increasingly gaining access to mobile phones, the power is increasingly being placed into the hands of individual consumers. To reach these consumers and stand out in the world wide web of competition, the core of the conversation is shifting away from enterprises wanting to translate a story toward creating an original one that will resonate with their audiences to create a more memorable experience.

This rush towards more content puts in stark contrast the fact that creating content (and locally relevant user experiences) just isn't some clients' core competence. Unsurprisingly, LSPs are rising to the occasion. Some have, for example, embedded creative teams within their business to create multilingual content for clients, others have set up content development and SEO teams in different geographies, and others again are even talking about transitioning from LSP to Content Provider or Global Content Partner. Taking a closer look, this transition does not seem too out of place. LSPs are already deeply embedded in the content journey due to the nature of translation work, which requires them to be aware of content related matters. So, this might just be a rather natural next step.

A similar development that confirms the increased focus on the end-user can be found in the discussions around Experiential Localization Quality Assessment, short xLQA. Language Quality Assurance (LQA) or Language Quality Assessment has been around for a long time and is an integral part of the translation process. It's the review process that measures the quality of the localized content, a task that is traditionally highly customized and aimed at finding mistakes.

Nimdzi's theory is that while LQA is important, end-users don't think in terms of localization quality of a product — they think in terms of their own experience using that product (presumably in their native language). Accuracy and traditional quality metrics are still important, but they are no longer relevant in isolation. Rather than wholly replace traditional quality practices, xLQA is an additional step, designed to measure the relationship between language quality and the end-customer's experience.

Which brings us back to what clients want. Much like end-users, enterprise buyers do not care about translation and localization in and of itself. What they *do*, however, care about is reaching their end-customers in the most impactful way possible, and ideally in one that is both cost optimizing and revenue generating.

Looking at the industry at large, what we can expect is a move toward two primary service levels:

01 Machine translation, AI, and automation for anything that is more technical, repetitive, and can be automated in an effort to increase efficiencies, decrease costs, and combat the increase in volumes and shorter turnaround times.

02 High-end content creation and creative services, tailored to reach specific audiences in specific markets. Not only for the overall creative service and marketing sector but also for services in highly regulated industries like Life Sciences.

A stronger partnership through consulting and insights

All too often, translation and localization are still being viewed as a cost factor and a commodity rather than an international revenue enabler. So, in an effort to increase their value proposition, many LSPs have started offering consulting and data-based insights to their clients, advising them on topics such as which markets they should go into, which technology is the best fit for them, and how to manage their digital channels. Quite naturally, this is creating a stronger partnership and more "stickiness."

This is also mirrored in the fact that large LSPs are increasingly moving away from project-based contracts and rather entering into multi-year master service agreements with their clients. In the same vein, interviewed LSPs mentioned a very **strong push for vendor consolidation on the client side**. While this might be good news for some LSPs, it might put smaller LSPs in a less favorable position. Even some of the larger players are noticing that the consolidation trend is not without its challenges, for instance, when high volumes of work are then being pushed onto fewer vendors.

Another development that is strengthening the partnership between LSP and enterprise buyers is that **buyers are increasingly outsourcing anything that is not part of their core competency**, mostly as a result of tighter budgets. Especially tasks like content creation, content review, and technology review are then being handed over to LSP partners. In the same vein, a few LSPs reported clients wanting to take a different approach to LQA and moving away from having inhouse teams handle this task. Instead, they are turning to their LSP partners, asking them to set up internal quality teams for them.

Going beyond language services

Much of what we are describing above is LSPs broadening their portfolio and adding adjacent services. What we mean by that are services that do not traditionally fall under the definition of *language* services, but are complementary to the LSP's offerings and allow them to provide their clients with a more complete package.

In the same vein, when the topic of M&A arose in conversations with the top 100, a number of companies expressed an interest in acquiring businesses outside the language services market — companies from industries that do not operate in the localization space but are complementary enough to offer a stepping stone to widen the reach of an LSP and to branch out into other sectors.

The new LSP

Now, where is the red thread in all of this?

Enterprise buyers are placing a much stronger emphasis on reaching their end-users. To achieve this goal, they want content that is more closely tailored to their consumers in order to maximize the impact of their products and services. As a result, LSPs see a growing demand for original content creation, and developments like these push LSPs into offering more adjacent services in order to solidify their position in their clients' supply chain. As the bonds between LSP and enterprise buyer strengthen, they evolve into a true, strategic partnership, which is also mirrored in clients choosing to work with fewer vendors on the basis of master service agreements.

In other words, as enterprise clients are trying to get closer to their end-users, LSPs are getting closer to *their* clients and are forming stronger business relationships through consulting, strategic advisory, and services that fall outside the area of language services. As a result, LSPs are widening their scope and enhancing their value proposition.

Dawn of the Multilingual Meeting Provider

Since the onset of the pandemic, the demand for video conferencing has gone through the roof. While platforms like Zoom, Microsoft Teams, and Webex were already being used prior to March 2020, the pandemic took things to a whole new level as video conferencing became the norm in, more or less, every area of society — from businesses to governments to schools to the average Joe and Jane, no matter what age group, no matter the setting (weddings, birthday parties, and funerals included).

But sooner or later the now well-known "Zoom-fatigue" started to set in and so people were trying to find ways to make their virtual meetings more engaging, and started exploring new features and meeting formats. In addition, accessibility and inclusivity increasingly moved into the focus at enterprises and public entities alike. Because for the first time, it was easier than ever to make meetings accessible for everyone no matter the location.

This development that suddenly brought language services to the forefront and into a top-of-mind position for new clients who had never used any kind of language services before was expressed in many different ways. For instance, once virtual events started to gain momentum, interpreting providers not only saw a spike in requests for remote interpreting but also for multilingual live captioning on various event platforms and for document translations for online meetings.

At the same time, LSPs who predominantly focus on translation and localization started receiving more requests for various types of remote interpreting (especially remote simultaneous interpreting), as well as for multilingual live captioning for virtual events.

What this development has shown is that there is a clear need in the market for a **Multilingual Meeting Provider (MMP)**. Yes, many companies already describe themselves as facilitating multilingual meetings — and they do. However, what we typically see in the market are either companies offering RSI *or* VRI, live captioning *or* machine interpreting, or a combination of a few of these services. Interviews with market players show that the needs of clients are shifting and buyers are increasingly looking for a provider that can do it all. Clients don't want to go to one company for their interpreting needs, to another for translation and again to another for captioning — and potentially all for the same event — especially as more types of new meetings are emerging all the time. What they want is one provider that can facilitate all their requirements for virtual multilingual meetings and events. Who is going to fill this current gap and in what way (through partnerships, acquisitions, building or buying new tech, adding services, etc.) remains to be seen.

Spotlight on industry segments

The language services industry offers many types of services and operates in even more verticals. In this section, we provide a more in-depth overview and analysis of a number of sectors within the industry that stood out in 2021 and that will continue to be the most relevant going into 2022.

AI and localization: Keeping up with the Joneses

We've hit a curious patch in the language services industry. A lot of the talk is still centered around the usual topics — MT is definitely one of the evergreen ones — but the industry at large is scrambling to come up with new ideas. Certainly, there are new trends popping up, some of which are here to stay (e.g. LSPs diversifying their portfolios with creative services such as content generation). With some external trends (*cough* metaverse *cough*), we're still waiting to see whether they will have any impact at all. Yet there is one buzzword that people ought to talk more about — AI. They have, but perhaps not often enough or maybe not in the right context. Only a handful of players in our industry have thus far found consistent success in this area. But AI should be talked about more — and here's why.

AI is ubiquitous. It's present in devices we use every day, whether we turn on Netflix, listen to Spotify, or ask Siri to find us the nearest restaurant so we can order takeout. The next decade figures to be one where more and more end-clients hop onto the AI bandwagon. So what does this mean for the language services industry? More work trickling down to LSPs, to begin with.

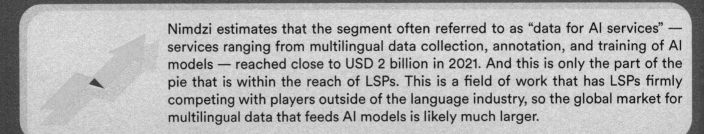

Nimdzi estimates that the segment often referred to as "data for AI services" — services ranging from multilingual data collection, annotation, and training of AI models — reached close to USD 2 billion in 2021. And this is only the part of the pie that is within the reach of LSPs. This is a field of work that has LSPs firmly competing with players outside of the language industry, so the global market for multilingual data that feeds AI models is likely much larger.

In other words, it's a pretty penny, with growing client demand and significant budgets to compete for. As we mentioned elsewhere in this report, LSPs looking to diversify their service offerings should keep an eye out for opportunities to solidify their status in their clients' eyes. The barrier to entry in the field of data-related services may be high, though. Let's take stock of a few key characteristics of this subsegment of the larger language services market and where it's headed:

- While it's all about how companies can smartly leverage the potential of AI, data for AI services is very much a human-in-the-loop type of service. Humans set up and maintain the tech platforms, pilot the programs, and do the actual collecting of the data. Data programs built for clients can span across several years and can mobilize thousands of resources with often very low ramp-up time before production starts. This requires quasi-continuous workforce management to find the right people, keep them engaged and mitigate attrition.

- Some LSPs have been doing this for quite a while, while some are just entering the playing field. Their technological savviness underpins their ability to perform the work. LSPs need to engage with their clients in a competent manner — and this may require a type of resource that isn't necessarily native to the language services ecosystem, such as computational scientists or natural language processing (NLP) specialists. This may push some LSPs out of their comfort zones. But the opportunity is too good to pass up.

- Big tech companies and e-commerce players are the ones driving the demand. Areas such as data for search engines or speech recognition are some of the main sources of work, but the proliferation of voice assistants and virtual chatbots in areas such as healthcare, banking, or travel may present appealing opportunities for LSPs. There's definitely more — one aspect to consider is that we, the humans, are barely scratching the surface of what different AI applications can do. Future demand is likely to soar beyond what we're seeing today.

- And here comes an advantage LSPs may have over pure tech players. LSPs have the multilingual background that gives them the edge when talking to clients, most of whom will predominantly reason in English (for example, the US remains the hotbed for AI investments). The ability of LSPs to deliver services across a multitude of languages, honed over time by hundreds and thousands of classic localization projects, shouldn't be understated.

- You may think this type of service is only for the big LSPs. While it may be true that their size allows them to respond to a critical requirement of data projects — scale — there is enough diversity in projects of varied scope and size for any LSP to develop competence in this area. As more industries hop onto the AI bandwagon and realize how data-hungry AI is, someone will need to fill the demand. Fortune may favor those few bold LSPs who dare to make the jump.

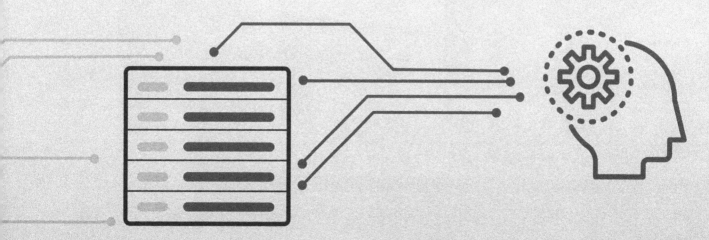

Interpreting: From onsite to remote to mainstream

First things first. Let's not beat around the bush and get right to it: **remote interpreting is here to stay**. The pandemic created the framework for people who resisted remote interpreting to embrace it and now that the genie is out of the bottle, it's hard to go back.

Does this mean the end of onsite interpreting? Of course not. There will always be scenarios in which it is preferable to have an interpreter onsite. For instance, when dealing with high-stakes clients, in end-of-life cases, in mental health settings, or when dealing with children, to name but a few. However, it does mean that the market for interpreting services has changed and will not go back to the way it was prior to March 2020.

 We estimate that the global interpreting market reached USD 9.1 billion in 2021 due to an exceptionally strong year. Considering the ongoing boom and changed landscape in the interpreting field, we have adjusted the compound annual growth rate (CAGR) for this segment to 6.5%. Taking this into consideration, the interpreting industry will reach USD 9.7 billion in 2022 and be valued at USD 12.5 billion by 2026.

The graph below shows the estimated market split between onsite and (the various types of) remote interpreting before the pandemic, at the height of the pandemic, and after the pandemic.

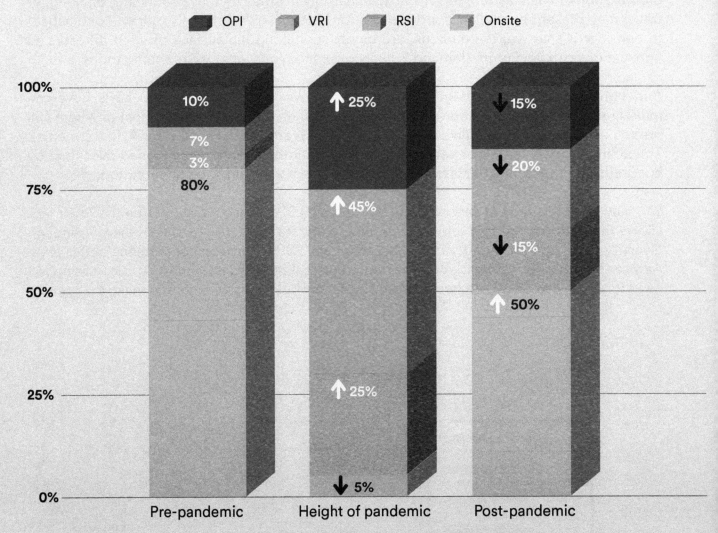

* OPI = Over-the-phone interpreting; VRI = Video remote interpreting, RSI = Remote simultaneous interpreting

An emerging trend that should be included in the last bar (bleeding into both the percentages for onsite and for RSI) is hybrid meetings, where some participants are onsite and some join a conference or meeting remotely. We can expect to see a lot more of these types of meetings in the post-pandemic future. In our current estimate, hybrid meetings will make up between 10 and 20% of the market in the years to come.

Remote simultaneous interpreting: Catching a ride on the Zoom boom

Prior to the pandemic, remote simultaneous interpreting (RSI) was a real niche within the language services industry. However, once the pandemic hit and all types of meetings, conferences, and events pivoted to the virtual world, RSI suddenly was in high demand. This demand is coming both from existing clients who have more virtual meetings than before and from new clients in different industries. Suddenly everyone is receiving requests for RSI.

This is not only reflected in the millions of dollars that RSI platforms have received in various investment rounds over the past two years, but also in the growing number of new RSI platforms. Looking at our Language Technology Atlas, the "RSI and conference interpreting" category grew from 20 to 34 different solutions in 2021. Projections indicate that it is not going to stop here. A number of traditional LSPs in the interpreting sector are thinking about building their own RSI platforms, and some VRI platforms are looking to partner with RSI tech players in an effort to meet their clients' changing needs and cash in on the trend.

A likely explanation for the RSI boom is the popularity of Zoom and similar platforms. The increased exposure to virtual meetings and events appears to have triggered a heightened interest in making these meetings more accessible — through multilingual captions and through RSI.

In fact, Zoom is the de facto largest RSI platform judging by the number of meetings. This might be controversial for some in the language industry but shouldn't really come as too big of a shock given its position in the wider conferencing market. While it is true that Zoom's main focus is not on multilingual meetings, the platform does have an RSI feature. The feature is more rudimentary as compared to specialized RSI platforms and is lacking some functionalities (e.g. relay and interpreter handover), but it works and is often what clients want.

The exposure to Zoom and the increased use of RSI has also had an interesting side effect, namely that interpreting has gone more mainstream. Originally fairly limited to conference interpreting (its field of origin), the pandemic has opened the door to new RSI clients. For instance, LSPs suddenly received requests for RSI for parent-teacher conferences and other school events. Local governments reached out wanting to add RSI to their town hall meetings and COVID-19 announcements. Educators from various fields, including healthcare education, have added RSI to their classes, and at least one large e-sports company is looking to add RSI to its virtual live events.

However, RSI is not the only area where the mainstream move can be observed. It holds true across different segments of the interpreting market. For instance, numerous vaccine centers across the US are equipped with portable, on-demand VRI devices (e.g. from AMN Language Services), and Walgreens pharmacies are partnering with VRI platform VOYCE to enable efficient communication between customers and employees (including language access for the Deaf and hard of hearing through sign language interpreting).

Media and gaming:
One more year of stirring up the crowds

Breaking growth records in the media localization space

Last year's forecast was correct — after a delay in production caused by the pandemic, content creation would speed up again during 2021, meaning that the video assets to be localized would grow exponentially. And that's just what happened. With the news of Netflix's localization volumes (seven million minutes of subtitled content and five million minutes of dubbed content in 2021), we can get a sense of what we're looking at — more than 13 years of subtitled content, and almost 10 years of dubbed content. And our industry delivered this huge amount of work in months. Moreover, this represents only figures from Netflix, which isn't even the biggest streaming platform out there. Add Disney+, Prime Video, Apple TV, HBO Max, and so on. Crazy, right? At the same time, it's not just the number of hours of content, but also the number of languages. In the past, the standard was 12 languages, now it's more than double that. This all adds to pre-production and post-production times for dubbing and subtitling.

The media industry is bigger than ever before and the growth of media localization companies in our ranking confirms this.

 On average, media localization agencies grew 24% in 2021 compared to 2020. The growth is mainly coming from the content created by the streaming platforms rather than traditional media such as broadcasters or movies for cinemas only.

That's why companies focusing on video on demand platforms are growing faster than the ones serving the broadcasting industry. This is also due to the fact that streaming platforms buy more distribution-related services from their providers besides subtitling and dubbing.

As opposed to 2020, where M&A activities had a big impact on the revenue increase, this year's growth is more organic in the media space. At the same time, this vertical is attracting the attention of investing firms, as we learned in early 2022 when Iyuno announced yet another round of funding from the Korean investment firm IMM Investments Corp.

This is all great news for the media localization industry but it doesn't come without downsides. Rapid growth can also lead to **scalability problems and talent crunch, which are two of the main challenges reported by the big players in this space**. Making sure that the growth is manageable without failing to meet clients' expectations is not always easy. This industry is highly creative so automation is not always possible compared to other more regulated industries such as legal or life sciences. Big players are making use of technology but, at the end of the day, this industry is very human-dependant on so many levels — not only are specialized translators and subtitlers limited but also voice talents, artistic directors, script adaptators, and specialized sound engineers. The growth is outpacing the growth of the workforce because the demand is increasing so fast — we're in a period of hypergrowth. Technology such as MT or synthetic voices can help to a certain extent, but it's not there yet to really help with the scalability challenge. **We simply need more people in the media localization industry.**

Apart from streamlining processes and technology, there are two more human solutions to the challenge of scalability and talent crunch:

01 Investing more in education.

02 Increasing rates to not only attract talent but also retain it.

Collaboration between the industry and academia is necessary to fill the gap and train a prepared workforce. Several companies are initiating some education-related projects. One way to make sure media localization companies get the best talent is to pay more than their competitors. To do so, they will need to renegotiate rates with clients — an overarching trend we discussed earlier in this report (see "The Great Renegotiation"). And the same applies to media companies. If they want to get the best teams, they need to pay more and renegotiate with their internal stakeholders. It is estimated that just between 0.1% and 1% of the budgets of film and show production goes into localization, so hopefully there's some room for negotiation. **Lowering rates is not an option anymore, and not increasing them is also unsustainable in the long run. Rates need to go back to what is fair for such a hyperspecialized service that requires technical skills, creativity and experience.**

The gaming industry is leading the way

Even if media companies are breaking records, gaming is the one (still) leading the way. Video games seem to be everywhere these days, attracting the attention of mainstream media and industries alike. The metaverse, virtual reality, IPs going transmedia, and big tech companies investing in gaming are some of the examples of why gaming is still the coolest kid on the block.

The metaverse seems to be something new and disruptive for many people outside the gaming sphere, but if you are old enough to remember Habbo Hotel or Second life, you will see so many similarities. Too many actually. And that's bad. The current metaverse is like playing a game on a PlayStation One. Games have evolved so much since then, and Fortnite offers a way better metaverse experience than some of the old-fashioned looking metaverses that are emerging these days. Living a more engaging and complex virtual life is probably something we will experience in the near future, but if we're going to do this, let's not reinvent the wheel but rather follow the lead of experts in virtual lives — gamers.

The media industry is hungry for more ideas for stories. Films based on games are nothing new. We have Mortal Kombat, Street Fighter, Tomb Raider, Resident Evil, Prince of Persia, and many more. This continues to be a trend but one that's even stronger than before. Last year we saw the launch of a world-wide phenomenon: the Netflix Original show Arcane, set in the universe of the competitive game *League of Legends* by Riot Games. This may be a sign of an effort from streaming platforms to attract the attention of Generation Alpha, who are basically living in their own metaverses already. The Uncharted film was recently released in cinemas, and HBO will air a show based on The Last of Us sometime in 2023. Transmedia seems to be a trend in entertainment that will follow in the upcoming years. That means more complex and multilayered user experiences.

Big tech companies have increasingly shown more interest in gaming as well. Amazon Games has been running since 2012, and they have recently announced that they will give free games to Prime subscribers, probably to increase engagement. Microsoft bought Blizzard-Activision last year, strengthening their position in the gaming space. Apple launched their video game subscription service, Apple Arcade, in 2019. And Netflix announced their game division at the end of 2021. With all these recent moves, we can just reaffirm the belief that the future of the game industry is, indeed, very bright.

How are these microtrends impacting localization, you might ask? Let's look at the numbers. Keywords Studios, the biggest player in the game localization space, grew around 40% in 2021 compared to 2020, which is a big jump. Of course, their revenues don't come only from localization, but the same comment could be applied to the rest of the biggest LSPs — they don't only offer translations, but a wide range of adjacent services to meet their clients' needs. LSPs are not only localization providers, but partners for global operations. Keywords envisioned this idea of becoming a single platform to meet all outsourcing needs of game developers. And they seem to be having success with this approach so far.

All in all, the consequences of the evolution of gaming will in one way or another impact localization operations. Companies that are not purely gaming-oriented entering the gaming space will bring new ways of working to the already established game localization workflows. For example, asking for more target languages, for more services, bigger word counts, faster turnaround times and so on. This might also pose an operational challenge for enterprises who will have to diversify their vendor pool looking for specialization, and they might have different teams working on the same IPs but on different platforms — one show on Netflix and one game on Xbox. Consistency in terminology, a renewed focus on account management, and also the user experience in general will be objectives to work toward. This year, and in the years to come, we will face exciting challenges in scalability, operations and usage of technology to cater for a delightful user experience in games and media.

Technology trends: MT and data

Over the last year, Nimdzi participated in various projects with LSPs looking to up their MT game. Through the conversations and consultancy sessions, we have seen LSPs tackle projects such as implementing year-long MT programs, experimenting with customization and MTPE dashboards, deciding on compensation and effort calculation, playing around MT for fuzzy matches. But what about the buyers?

Overall, for 2021, several distinct studies confirmed that what many users want is ease-of-use — being automatically presented with the most suitable MT option for their particular use case. Enterprise-level customers mostly would like not to worry about understanding MT quality metrics, evaluating and comparing MT engines, setting up API keys, or tracking the engines' performance. Some believe it is the job of the LSP or a collaboration between the provider of the translation management system (TMS), the MT provider, and the LSP.

As we noted in the last edition of the Language Technology Atlas, if companies are looking for high-quality results, they need to invest time in nurturing AI tools from the start: from creating and preparing datasets to technically rolling out a customization initiative at a given enterprise. This is one of the catalysts for the recent developments around MT and data — tech companies as well as modern LSPs have been making an effort to bring secure MT closer to enterprise users. This is also reflected in LSPs developing their own TMX editors to help clean data for MT.

Today's data-driven MT relies on two basic principles:

01 The companies need to invest in training the MT engine with quality human-annotated data, so it can learn to do a better job with the new languages and domains.

02 The data needs to be cleaned up in order for the machine learning algorithms to be able to work with it.

LSPs, therefore, are hiring more annotators and investing more in data-centric services, sometimes even coming up with special concepts like AI localization (by Pactera EDGE).

Speaking of initiatives around data, Intento MT Studio has released Enhanced Data Cleaning (as well as new metric options). In addition, Intento integrated the entire workflow into one interface, taking away the need to import or export data throughout the project. This is another illustration of tech players bringing MT closer to the user.

In addition to the language technology companies that already help with MT customization (starting with USD 3K per engine), we're also seeing easier, "lighter" plug-and-play solutions around MT and data introduced by LSPs themselves: for example, LSPs launching their own platforms for data labeling.

Another recent example is TAUS' Data-Enhanced Machine Translation (DEMT). DEMT promises to deliver translation quality similar to the one achieved by post-editing of MT, but delivered virtually in real-time with "prices 50% to 80% lower than the "human-in-the-loop" service." In DEMT, users select a training dataset, upload a file for MT, then download the ready MT'd file. The BLEU score improvement for the selected dataset is visible prior to making the purchase.

Data has been a powerful driver for MT for several years, but it only recently gained enough momentum to make it a viable option for more LSPs. To summarize, one of the notable trends in MT and data is the IT/LSP symbiosis around enterprise-friendly MT and data solutions.

When it comes to more classic MTPE scenarios, where a professional post-editor (or two) polishes up an MT output, another way of pricing MTPE is picking up steam. Namely, effort-based compensation for human linguists, which is already available in the business models of Lionbridge and Tilde, as well as facilitated by Memsource. Effort-based costs for MTPE, where linguists are compensated for the calculated effort spent on post-editing, can be significantly lower than in a regular scenario — paying for each new word but with an MT discount.

Geographies

North
America
35.8%

Where the largest LSPs are

Out of 165 medium-to-large-sized companies identified in 2021, 41.8% are headquartered in Europe and 35.8% in North America. Companies from Asia represent 18.8% of the geographical distribution. Australia & New Zealand host 3.6% of the top players. Africa and South America have not yet produced an LSP that could be included in the Nimdzi 100. There is only one company from the Middle East that has made it into our ranking, and for the second year in a row (BLEND).

Compared to 2020, there is a slight decrease in companies headquartered in North America (37.3% in 2020) and Asia (19.6% in 2020). This difference is made up for by a larger number of LSPs based in Europe and Australia & New Zealand (only 39.9% and 3.3% in 2020 respectively).

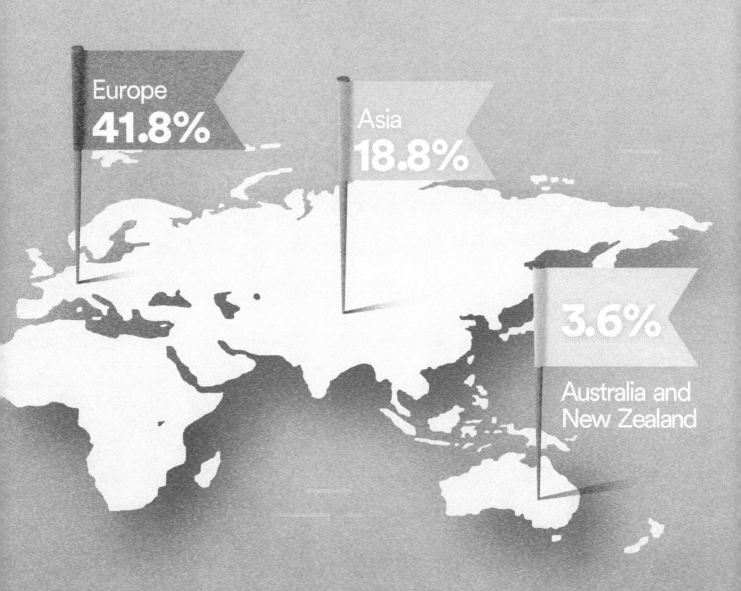

Europe
41.8%

Asia
18.8%

3.6%
Australia and New Zealand

Where the clients are

We asked survey respondents to indicate the percentage of their revenue derived from customers based in different parts of the world. The results show that in 2021, North America was the region with the largest client base in the industry, followed by Europe and Asia. While the market distribution is similar to the one we observed in 2020, the weight shifted slightly and North America reclaimed its top position from Europe which had the largest client base in 2020.

As the map shows, 41.1% of revenues in 2021 came from clients based in Europe, down from 48.9% in 2020. This slight decline in the European client base seems to have shifted to North America. In 2021, North America accounted for 45.0% of the client base, up from 33.9% in 2020.

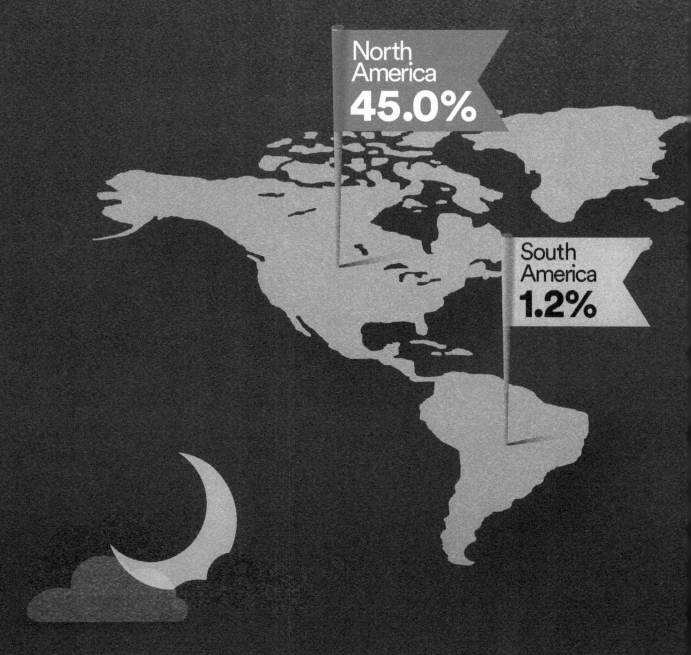

North America
45.0%

South America
1.2%

Given that the US is the largest market for language services by revenue, it makes sense that the majority of clients are based in this region. What might also add to the slight shift we are seeing are increasingly strict regulations in Europe, which may deter LSPs from entering these markets.

Revenues amounting to 12.0% were derived from customers in Asia in 2021 as compared to 14.7% in 2020. Same as in 2020, South America (1.2%), Australia (0.4%), and Africa (0.3%), are the smallest regions in terms of client base in 2020.

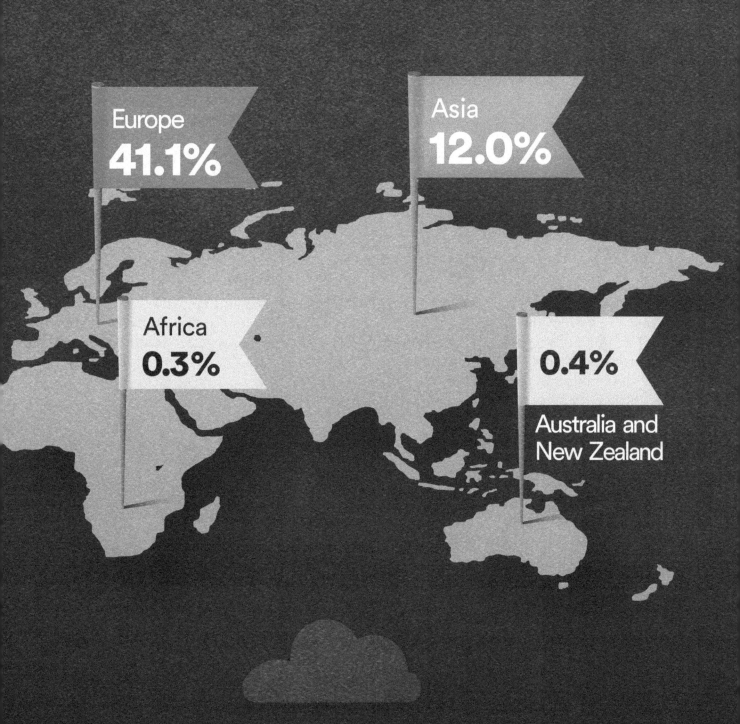

Europe
41.1%

Asia
12.0%

Africa
0.3%

0.4%
Australia and
New Zealand

Turning the page after COVID-19

Throughout 2021, the world continued to deal with COVID-19 in waves. Life seemed to return to relative normalcy for extended periods of time, but people were still faced with lockdowns and restrictions as case numbers surged. Experiences have been far from uniform across the world, but one thing has been consistent: unpredictability.

Experiences in the business world have been just as varied. Certainly, just about every company was affected in some way by COVID-19, but across different regions, different industries, and different companies sizes, the opportunities and challenges were diverse. Some people have continued to work remotely; others have returned to face-to-face service delivery. Many industries saw new or continuing growth as we emerged from the pandemic; others have not yet made a full recovery. Ultimately though, everyone has settled into the 'new normal', and life has gone on.

Where last year we unpacked how the language industry was impacted by the pandemic, this year we explored the post-COVID experiences and what the path forward might look like.

So how *is* recovery from COVID-19 looking so far?

It's no secret that many companies took a hit in the first half of 2020. However, as we reported in last year's edition of the Nimdzi 100, recovery was already evident in the industry by the end of 2020. This trend has continued, with **a whopping 90% of our survey respondents reporting that their business has now gotten back to pre-COVID-19 levels**. Of those yet to fully recover, 50% expect to see this happen in 2023.

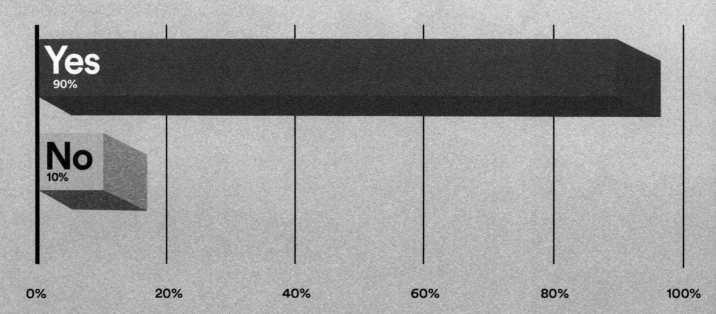

Profitability has also boomed since 2020 — another very promising sign that the industry is on the right track. Only 8.5% of companies reported decreased profitability in 2021, down from almost 19% last year, and the number of companies that reported increased profitability rose from 45.5% to 66.7%.

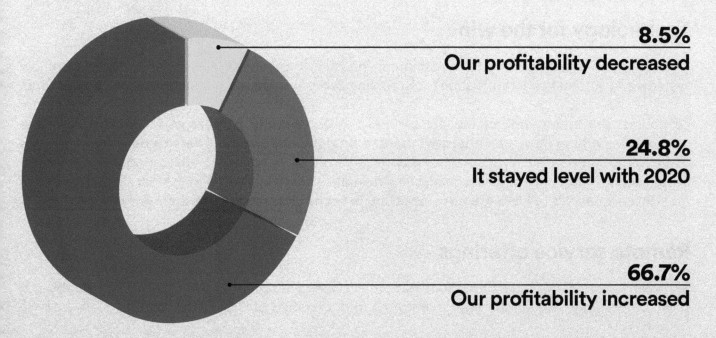

8.5%
Our profitability decreased

24.8%
It stayed level with 2020

66.7%
Our profitability increased

The nitty-gritty numbers also add gravity to these figures. On average, in 2021 profitability increased by an impressive 56.2%, while the average decrease in productivity was only -14.7%. The results from our survey also show that, of companies yet to return to their pre-COVID-19 levels, only one company reported decreased profitability in the past year.

Remote work: Here to stay?

As predicted last year, the vast majority of companies (75%) have embraced the advantages of remote work, offering a hybrid model for employees moving forward. What this looks like in practice will differ from company to company. Interestingly, the remaining companies are split exactly equally, with half reporting that they will continue to work predominantly online, and half saying they are either back in the office already or are currently planning their return.

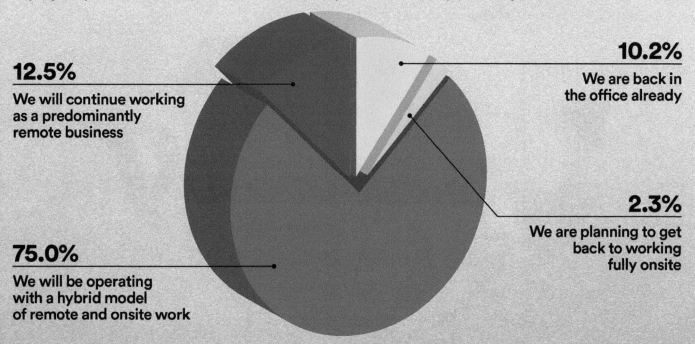

10.2%
We are back in the office already

12.5%
We will continue working as a predominantly remote business

2.3%
We are planning to get back to working fully onsite

75.0%
We will be operating with a hybrid model of remote and onsite work

The most popular growth strategies coming out of the pandemic

Technology for the win

'Technology' is a pretty broad term within our industry. It encompasses everything from workflow systems and automation to translation tools, service delivery solutions, machine learning, and beyond.

Of course, the importance of technology and the opportunity it presents for language service providers is nothing new, and, after two years of predominantly remote service delivery, it perhaps comes as no surprise that its importance is currently front-of-mind for growth strategists. In any case, overall acknowledgment of it as a catalyst for revenue growth increased in the last 12 months. **More than three-quarters of LSPs are now investing in technology as part of their growth strategy.**

Remote service offerings

Surprise, surprise. We're talking about remote services yet again. We'll stop harping on about it soon, but it really wouldn't be right to ignore it in the context of COVID-19, right?

Out of all the new requests that companies received over the past year, remote services were named most frequently. Remote interpreting (especially VRI) is, perhaps unsurprisingly, the most common of these, but survey respondents also reported new requests for virtual event management and e-learning solutions. Companies that already offered these services had a natural advantage at the beginning of the pandemic. However, we are now seeing strategic expansion into these areas by other companies who want to take advantage of the new demand.

Whether this demand will endure once the world returns to more in-person activities and events, however, remains to be seen.

Business expansion

Perhaps the clearest trend among survey respondents this year was LSPs embracing new opportunities to expand their business by venturing into new markets, verticals, and service lines.

To illustrate, in the past year, **64.2% of companies have added new services** (by contrast, only 40.7% are actively focusing on their core competencies), **54.3% are looking to expand into new markets** (double the number of companies that are focusing on their domestic market), and **49.4% have diversified their client base**.

It is reasonable to assume that the pandemic-driven increase in remote services and solutions has helped make international expansion more attractive and achievable. Especially for smaller LSPs, who may not have had the financial muscles to establish a physical presence in multiple regions.

Sales

As was the case in 2020, companies continued to invest in sales and marketing throughout 2021. Roughly seven in ten companies have added new sales channels (14.8%), expanded sales and marketing teams (35.8%), or done both (22.2%). Investing in sales has always been a smart growth strategy, and this is especially true today. The industry has been through some exciting but massive changes, so a solid sales team is critical to continue driving growth and supporting clients in such an unpredictable environment.

Hypes and buzzwords: Just smoke and mirrors?

In a diverse industry, it can sometimes feel like the list of trends is endless. New hypes are springing up all the time, but which ones are worth paying attention to and which ones are just smoke and mirrors?

The metaverse

Let's start with what is probably the most hyped trend in early 2022 — the metaverse. What the metaverse promises is to be the future of the internet, which will provide a completely immersive experience in the virtual world and one where everyone and everything is connected. So far so good. While some hype it as the next best thing after sliced bread and a place with unlimited business opportunities, others question if the metaverse is really that different from the internet we already have today.

One example that illustrates the opportunities the metaverse holds well, is the fashion industry. Already, fashion brands are making millions of dollars by selling virtual items of clothing in the metaverse. Not for people to wear, but for their avatars — or even better, selling both the real item and the virtual item so that the person and their avatar are perfectly matched (a new trend). In addition, high-end fashion brands are putting on virtual fashion shows.

To some reading this, the idea of paying for virtual clothing might sound crazy. For others it might sound like the sky's the limit as far as business opportunities are concerned. But for others — namely gamers — it might just sound like yesterday's news.

It is estimated that three billion people in the world regularly play video games and that gaming has become the leading form of entertainment across all age groups. The metaverse has grown out of gaming, and in the gaming world it certainly is nothing new to buy virtual items. In fact, gamers around the world spend over USD 100 billion a year on virtual goods.

So, what does this mean for the localization industry? One thing is certain and that is that more content always means more demand for localization services down the line. If brands are selling to end-users in the metaverse, the same rules apply as in any other localization scenario: global brands that want to provide a truly personalized experience that reaches people, need to speak to consumers in their own languages.

Will this disrupt the localization industry? Hardly. It may very well be that what happens in the metaverse just translates into yet another different format of content that can be funneled into "classic" localization workflows. For the language services industry the key may not be to try and picture all that is possible in the metaverse (much of which we cannot yet fully wrap our brains around anyway), but rather to keep a close eye on adoption and adjacent tech trends (e.g. VR or AR headsets) so that they are ready when clients inevitably come calling, asking to localize their own specific version of the metaverse experience.

Continuous localization

Continuous localization has become one of those buzzwords that seems to continuously pop up in conversations across the industry. The question, however, is — is it really (still) that different from localization? Isn't it rather that these days, continuous localization is what localization has evolved into? Similarly to the way that neural machine translation (NMT) is just the latest version of machine translation (MT)?

Five years ago continuous localization still meant something in the sense that it was not the norm yet and made for something to advertise and brag about. However, these days it is more or less expected that a localization program will be continuous and agile.

What continuous localization should also imply is some form of tech enabled workflow that allows for a high number of handoffs, no minimum fees, and low word counts. For instance, instead of weekly handoffs with 10,000 words, it's 10 handoffs per day, each with 200 words.

Windows 95 was sold in a box at your local consumer electronics store. Today, Windows updates constantly via the internet and localization has adapted to that. With content coming at us, the consumers, hard and fast from every angle in an uninterrupted flow, continuous localization may very well be the new default setting.

Sustainability: Is Green the next ISO?

As the dangers related to the climate crisis are becoming more tangible, the topic is increasingly moving into the focus of public debate, and activists around the globe are urging governments to hold large corporations accountable for their share of the situation. Subsequently, what used to be a *nice-to-have* tag on a website or social media account might just become a *must-have*. In conversations with industry players, it has become clear that being sustainable is becoming a key consideration in companies' strategy in order to attract more clients.

Green policies, environmental initiatives, or ISO 14 001 mean that clients in a number of sectors need to have an effective environmental management system in place. These eco-friendly programs focus on making more environmentally conscious choices, including minimizing energy and water waste, reducing business waste, impact sourcing, supporting local communities, and many other activities.

What's more, global businesses insist that their partners and the whole supply chain follow the same or similar principles. Strong Corporate Social Responsibility (CSR) with a focus on sustainable business practices plays a vital role when potential clients are choosing their vendors. And, it doesn't end here — sustainability is not only an outward-facing strategy but an internal one as well, as people are increasingly looking for an employer with values similar to their own, who is socially and environmentally conscious. In times of the Great Resignation, this factor has become even more relevant.

These days, being sustainable is not just a badge of honor. Moving forward, it may become another requirement for companies to comply with. The question whether businesses go green for the sake of sustainability or the sake of higher profits still remains. Then again — does it really matter?

GPT-3

With all the talk of content creation, we would be remiss not to address the latest hype in this field — AI-generated content, specifically via OpenAI's latest model GPT-3 (stands for Generative Pre-trained Transformer 3). While more primitive language-generators have existed for a few years now, GPT-3 is hyped as a game changer. The language model which uses deep learning to produce human-like text can process 175 billion parameters (the previous version could handle 1.5 billion) and is predominantly intended as a tool to assist writers and solve the issue of writer's block.

Tests done to date, such as by a writer from the Washington Post, are admittedly impressive. So impressive in fact, that you might be forgiven for thinking that this is the answer to the mountains of requests for original content creation that are starting to pile up. But not so fast. While impressive, and at times eerily close to the style of the original authors the machine was fed with, GPT-3 is, for now, mostly geared toward fiction. Because, while the AI tool is good at style, it is lacking in substance. In that sense, it is more of a tool that enables writing rather than replaces writers.

Tests done by Nimdzi show that, at least for now, GPT-3 is not fit to produce any kind of content that has value for stakeholders in the language industry and its end clients. However, given the speed at which this kind of technology is evolving, the sky may just be the limit.

People-centric

A common theme identified on calls with LSPs of all sizes — whether that was during briefings for this report or other calls throughout the year — was that people are the biggest assets of any business. Similarly, when we interview leaders in the language industry for our C-Suite HotSeat show and ask what success means to them, the majority of C-level executives mention the well-being of their employees. It sounds like every employee's dream, but, how much of this is a reality and how much of it is just a buzzword?

There is a myriad of studies about mental health issues and burnout in the workplace. To name just two, a study by McKinsey found that almost half of all employees experience various levels of burnout, and a study by Deloitte with over one thousand respondents found that as many as 77% respondents reported having experienced burnout at their current job, mostly due to overwhelming levels of stress.

Considering statistics like these, one cannot help but wonder if anyone is actually acting on the people-centricity mantra that is being thrown around and praised so often. The language industry is a people-focused business and as we established earlier in this report, talent is becoming increasingly scarce. This makes you ask yourself: How people-centric is your business really? Who is brave enough to not just talk the talk but also walk the walk?

Where do we go from here?

The past two years have been chaotic and challenging but were also marked by innovation and ingenuity. While many LSPs struggled to adapt their business to the rapidly changing environment in 2020, our data show that in 2021 the industry reaped the rewards. In many areas, growth was accelerated beyond expectations, and as companies learned to adapt their business models and services to meet the new demands of buyers, the vast majority have not only simply recovered but rather have seen record growth over the past year.

LSPs who added new service lines or virtual platforms over the last two years are unlikely to take them down again post-pandemic. What this means is that these companies are now in a position to offer a wider range of services to their clients, thereby increasing the likelihood of both client retention as well as new customer acquisition.

The end of the COVID-19 pandemic is perhaps not in sight yet, but the biggest upheavals are behind us. The focus has shifted toward recovery and companies are working on solutions for the medium- and long-term future. Hopefully one with fewer blindsiding changes, but with just as much opportunity for ingenuity and innovation.